to

Marguerite and Frank

ACKNOWLEDGMENTS

Many people helped me in the course of writing this book and I am grateful to them all. Most of all, I thank Dr. Marguerite Potter, professor of British history at Texas Christian University, teacher, friend, and occasional devil's advocate, who gave so generously of her advice, criticism, and encouragement. I also wish to thank Peter Hammond, research officer of the Richard III Society, London, and Dr. Keith Odom, associate professor of English at Texas Christian University, who were kind enough to read the manuscript and offer valuable suggestions. The staff of the Mary Couts Burnett Library of Texas Christian University, particularly Mary Charlotte Faris, reference librarian, and others in the Reference and Inter-Library Loan departments, were most helpful in tracking down some of the more obscure sources used in this work. Finally, I thank my husband, Franklin, for his unfailing patience and encouragement.

TABLE OF CONTENTS

One

INTRODUCTION

On August 22, 1485, Richard III fell mortally wounded at Bosworth Field. Except for a few easily crushed rebellions led by Yorkist pretenders during the reign of Henry VII, that battle ended the Wars of the Roses. Hardly, however, had the crown settled comfortably on the brow of Henry Tudor than a war of words began which continues to this day. The weapons wielded by the antagonists in this conflict have been pen and ink rather than mace and sword and each combatant, whether professional or amateur, has been as totally committed to his cause as were those who fought and died for Lancaster or York in the years between 1455 and 1485.

The central figure in that long drawn-out controversy, Richard Plantagenet, was a slight, short, unprepossessing man, the last of the dynasty founded more than three hundred years earlier by Henry II. Richard has aroused more passionate hatred and scorn and has inspired more spirited defense than any other monarch in English history. Was he the monster of depravity immortalized by More and Shakespeare or the victim of a Tudor conspiracy as portrayed by Horace Walpole and many nineteenth- and twentieth-century writers? Was he, as his detractors charge, a misshapen hunchback who waded to the throne through the blood not only of his two innocent nephews, but also of a saintly king, his own wife, his brother, and other victims who stood in his path? Or, are there, as his defenders protest, other less dramatic but more convincing explanations of the events which enabled Richard to gain the crown? These are not questions which can be answered simply if, indeed, they can be answered at all. Nevertheless, for the past five hundred years many historians and writers of varying degrees of talent have attempted to resolve them.

In succeeding chapters we shall examine the origins and growth of the so-called Tudor myth in order to see how it shaped the thoughts and opinions of generations of British

1

and American historians.   There can be no doubt that most,
if not all, of the historians, playwrights, or novelists who
chose to write on this period were to some degree influenced
by the works of the Tudor chroniclers and historians.   It
seems evident that even those writers who consciously, and
often vehemently, rejected the basic Tudor premise were
subtly influenced by it.

For convenience and clarity both the fiction and non-
fiction works will be discussed chronologically.   In this way
the trends of historical opinion, however slight, may be more
easily discerned.   There has been no century since the fifteenth when interest in the subject of Richard III has been
lacking.   There were, however, long periods of time when
other, more pressing concerns turned men's minds from the
study of their past and these periods are, therefore, unproductive so far as the present subject is concerned.   The
greatest number of works, and the heating up of the controversy, date from the nineteenth century, and this interest has
continued, almost without abatement, to the present day.

Many writers of fiction have used the reigns of Edward IV, Edward V, and Richard III as the setting for their
novels and plays.   Some of these works are familiar to even
the most casual reader but many, on the other hand, are
relatively unknown.   In the chapters devoted to them their
value as history and their importance as opinion-shapers will
be examined.   While much of the material reviewed is well-
known, it is to be hoped that the discussions of lesser known
works will be of some interest, even though the importance
of those works in the controversy may have been slight.

Two

THE STRUGGLE FOR THE CROWN

Now is the winter of our discontent
Made glorious summer by this sun of York.
                              --Richard III I.i.

The controversy surrounding Richard III has centered
on several events, namely the deaths of Edward of Lancaster, Henry VI, George of Clarence, and the princes in the
Tower. Somewhat less controversial, but still the source of
much disagreement, were the deaths of Richard's wife, Anne
Neville, Anthony Woodville, and Lord Hastings. Many of the
facts concerning these deaths are clouded in uncertainty and
for this reason speculation about Richard's role in them has
flourished. Before turning to an examination and comparison
of the various views expounded by writers of history and fiction, a brief review of the known facts concerning the life and
career of Richard III might prove useful. [1]*

Richard was born on October 2, 1452, at Fotheringhay Castle. He was the twelfth of thirteen children born to
Richard, Duke of York, and his wife, Cicely Neville, and
the youngest of the seven who survived infancy. In this family of large, fair, healthy children the dark, undersized,
sickly Richard must have seemed like a changeling. During
the seven years he lived at Fotheringhay Richard had the
company only of his brother George, who was three years
his senior, and his sister Margaret, who was six years older than he. Edward and Edmund, the two oldest boys, lived
at Ludlow Castle in the Welsh Marches, while Anne and
Elizabeth, the older girls, were being trained in other noble
households according to the custom of the day. The children
saw their parents only rarely. [2]

Richard grew up in an unstable and dangerous period

---

*See Chapter Notes, beginning on page 113.

3

in English history. The old feudal system of loyalty based
on land tenure was crumbling and a new power, based on the
system of "livery and maintenance," was taking its place.
In return for the "good-lordship" of a powerful magnate, a
retainer promised his services in peace and war. Thus, the
lord had armed men when he needed them and the retainer
received protection against his enemies, wages in some
cases, and, all too frequently, immunity from punishment by
law. It was common practice during the fifteenth century
for powerful lords to threaten or bribe juries to find in their
favor. It was the sworn duty of the monarch to see that
justice was done, but during the reign of Henry VI this oath
had little meaning. Henry had frequent periods of madness
and the court was dominated by his beautiful and high-spirited
wife, Margaret of Anjou. She protected her partisans and
persecuted those whom she believed to be against her. She
treated Richard's father, the Duke of York, as her chief
enemy and so turned him into one. [3]

During the spring and summer of 1459 it was apparent
that the queen intended an all-out war against the Yorkists.
The Duke of York, fearing that Fotheringhay was no longer
safe, moved Margaret, George, and Richard to Ludlow, a
large, strongly fortified castle belonging to his family. It
was there that Richard met his two oldest brothers for the
first time. Edward, Earl of March was seventeen and Edmund, Earl of Rutland, was sixteen. [4]

Followers of York gathered that summer at Ludlow in
preparation for the attack they felt certain would come. In
October they learned that the king's army was at Coventry
and was marching toward Ludlow. The Yorkists sent Henry
a petition assuring him of their loyalty. He responded by
promising pardon to all who would desert the Yorkist cause. [5]

The duke's armies camped on Ludford Meadows and
prepared for battle. On the night of October 12 the best and
most experienced of the Yorkist troops, the Calais garrison
led by Andrew Trollope, deserted to the king, taking with
them the Yorkist battle plans. The duke and his sons, Edward and Edmund, and the Earl of Salisbury and his son, the
Earl of Warwick, fled to safety. The duchess and her two
younger boys remained behind and threw themselves on the
king's mercy. They reckoned without Queen Margaret's fury.
After the royal army had looted the castle and pillaged the
town of Ludlow as if it were enemy territory, the duchess
and her sons were taken to Coventry. York, Warwick, and

Salisbury were attainted by parliament and their estates declared forfeit. [6]

Meanwhile, the Duke of York and Edmund had sailed for Ireland where the Irish and Anglo-Irish rallied to their support. Indeed, the Irish were so loyal that they executed any man brave, or foolish, enough to bring a royal writ for York's arrest. [7] Warwick, Salisbury, and Edward had escaped to Calais which, fortunately for them, had remained true to its captain, Warwick. [8] Edward, concerned for the safety of his two younger brothers, wrote to the Archbishop of Canterbury to ask him to look after them. As a result, the boys were taken into the Archbishop's household where they remained from early 1460 until September of that year, when they rejoined their mother. [9]

On June 26, 1460, Warwick, Edward, and Salisbury landed with two thousand troops at Sandwich and went directly to London. They were welcomed by the city magistrates who lent them one thousand pounds, whereupon they marched north to meet the king's army, which was encamped south of Northampton. The treachery of some of the king's soldiers enabled the Yorkists to capture the king, who was then conducted to London in state. Following the establishment of a new government under firm Yorkist control, the Duchess of York, accompanied by George and Richard, arrived in London but the duchess soon left to join her husband who had landed in Chester. George and Richard, however, remained in London and not a day went by without a visit from Edward. It is quite likely that this loving attention from his older brother during this unsettled period in his life can explain Richard's lifelong devotion and loyalty to Edward. [10]

On October 10, the Duke of York returned to London. He went directly to Westminster where the lords were assembled, placed his hand on the throne, and announced that he had come to claim it by hereditary right. All of the peers, including Warwick and Edward, were shocked and dismayed by this action. [11] They wanted York to reform the government, not to seize the crown. Finally, after much legal debate, King Henry agreed that if he were permitted to keep the crown for life, the Duke of York would be his heir and would be named Protector. [12] This action disinherited Queen Margaret's son, something she would not countenance.

The infuriated queen fled north where she raised an
army by offering the Scots the border town of Berwick-on-
Tweed in return for their aid. [13] The Yorkists, meanwhile,
began to assemble their own armies and Edward went into
Wales to raise men. The Duke of York and the Earl of
Salisbury marched off to Yorkshire, leaving Warwick in London to run the government. On December 30, in violation
of a Christmas truce agreed to by both sides, the Lancastrian army attacked the Yorkists outside Sandal Castle near
Wakefield. York, his son Edmund, and Salisbury were slain
and their heads were taken to York and nailed up over the
Micklegate Bar. Margaret, never one to leave well enough
alone, had the duke's head adorned with a paper crown. [14]

By the death of his father, Edward became the Yorkist claimant to the throne. In February 1461, at Mortimer's
Cross, he defeated a large Lancastrian army but, a few days
later, at the second battle of St. Albans, Warwick was rout-
ed by the queen who succeeded in rescuing her husband from
Yorkist hands. The queen's forces followed the fleeing Yorkists to London, pillaging as they went. [15] The Duchess of
York, fearing for the lives of her two young sons should the
Lancastrian army take the city, sent them to Burgundy
where they were welcomed and royally treated by Duke
Philip. [16]

London, however, held out against the Lancastrians,
and when Edward entered the city on March 4, he was en-
thusiastically proclaimed king. [17] Thereupon, Margaret and
her army fled northward, pursued by the Yorkists. On
March 29, Palm Sunday, in a late, but fierce snowstorm,
the two armies met at Towton. In a bloody battle the out-
numbered Yorkists completely defeated the Lancastrian
army. [18] Henry, Margaret, and their son fled into Scotland.

When the news of the Yorkist victory reached Burgundy in mid-April, George and Richard were escorted to
Calais by a guard of honor. From there they went to the
Palace of Shene (Richmond) where their brother, King Edward IV, waited to greet them. Richard was not quite nine
years old, yet in his brief lifetime he had experienced
great danger and misfortune--the loss of his father, a brother, and an uncle, and virtual imprisonment and exile. Now,
under the protection of his handsome, gifted brother, fortune
for the first time appeared to smile on him.

On June 27 George and Richard, newly created

RICHARD III:
The Making of a Legend

by

Roxane C. Murph

The Scarecrow Press, Inc.

Metuchen, N. J.   1977

Library of Congress Cataloging in Publication Data

Murph, Roxane C
    Richard III : the making of a legend.

    Bibliography: p.
    Includes index.
    1. Richard III, King of England, 1452-1485.
2. Great Britain--Kings and rulers--Biography.
3. Richard III, King of England, 1452-1485, in fiction,
drama, poetry, etc.
DA260.M8   942.04'6'0924 [B]   77-4021
ISBN 0-8108-1034-4

Copyright © 1977 by Roxane C. Murph

Manufactured in the United States of America

Knights of the Bath, took part in the coronation of the new
king. Edward named George as the Duke of Clarence and
Richard as Duke of Gloucester, and both boys were made
Knights of the Garter.

The age of nine was none too soon to begin the cus-
tomary period of apprenticeship in the household of a great
noble in order to learn all the knightly accomplishments.
The king had decided that his brother Richard should enter
the household of the richest and most powerful nobleman in
England, his cousin the Earl of Warwick. Late in the year
1461 Richard went to the earl's great castle of Middleham
in Wensleydale to begin his training. [19] It was there that he
met Robert Percy and Francis Lovell who were also being
schooled in Warwick's household. These two youngsters became Richard's closest friends and remained, to the end of
their lives, his staunchest supporters. [20] The boys all lived
together and received instruction in Latin, law, mathematics,
music, religion, and the code of chivalric behavior and eti-
quette. Each day they practiced riding, hunting, and the use
of arms. In the evening they were taught to sing, dance,
and play musical instruments. Richard worked diligently on
all of his lessons, but his greatest effort was directed toward developing skill in the use of weapons. [21]

During the next few years the king heaped honors and
lands on his two brothers. At the age of twelve Richard
was appointed Commissioner of Array for nine counties and
charged with levying troops to clear Northumberland of Lancastrians. George, although he was three years older than
Richard, was not considered sufficiently mature for this responsibility, a fact which infuriated him. This, and other
incidents of this period which indicated Edward's favoritism
to Richard, may have marked the beginning of the hostility
which George later displayed toward both his brothers. [22]

In September 1464, Edward announced his marriage
to Elizabeth Woodville, a Lancastrian widow and the mother
of two young sons. [23] The marriage, which had been performed in great secrecy months before, was to have serious
and far-reaching consequences. Warwick had been negotiat-
ing a French marriage for the king and felt publicly humili-
ated by the king's action. This caused a breach between the
two strong-minded men. Warwick, who had helped his cousin Edward seize the throne, assumed he would be the power
behind it. Edward, however, intended to rule in fact as
well as name.

The strained relations between the king and kingmaker probably accounted for Edward's order, in the spring of 1465, that Richard be removed from Middleham. [24] Richard spent the next five years at Westminster in a court dominated by the relatives of the queen. The members of the Woodville clan were numerous, aggressive, and greedy, and it was not long before they had secured for themselves the greatest offices and the richest marriages in the kingdom. [25] The queen's sister Katherine was married to the Duke of Buckingham who was a dozen or more years her junior, while her twenty-year-old brother John captured the heart and hand of the eighty-year-old Dowager Duchess of Norfolk. It is not surprising that the queen and her family earned the enmity of the old nobility.

The resentment of Warwick, the head of the powerful Neville family, took a positive and dangerous form. He attempted to win the king's two brothers over to his side. Although Richard was no doubt flattered by the attentions showered on him, he recognized Warwick's treasonable intent and remained loyal to the king. Warwick had more success with George. In 1469, against the express command of the king, George of Clarence married Warwick's daughter, Isobel Neville, in a hurried and secret ceremony at Calais. [26] When they returned to England, Warwick gathered an army, captured the king, and executed several of the royal adherents, including the queen's father, her brother John, and the earls of Pembroke and Devon. [27]

Where was Richard during this period? Apparently the Nevilles considered him of such little ability and importance that he was not detained with his brother. When the king learned, however, that Richard and Lord Hastings had managed to raise armies to come to his rescue, he secretly summoned his Council to join him at Pontefract where he was being held prisoner. When the Council and the loyal armies appeared, Edward coolly informed his captors that these men had come to accompany him to London and he intended to go with them. [28]

This rescue caused the king to appreciate more fully the loyalty and ability of his youngest brother. On his return to London, Edward rewarded Richard by appointing him Constable of England for life. This was an extremely powerful position and carried with it great responsibility. The Constable, as President of the Court of Chivalry and Courts Martial, could determine and punish acts of treason. [29]

Richard was also appointed Chief Justice of North Wales for
life, and it was in this position that he undertook his first
independent military command. He quickly suppressed a
Welsh rebellion and recaptured the castles of Cardigan and
Carmarthen. Early in 1470 Richard became Chief Justice of
South Wales, which meant he was the virtual ruler of Wales.
He thus displaced Warwick who had taken these offices for
himself at the time he held the king captive. [30]

Despite a show of reconciliation between Warwick and
the king, the Nevilles continued to instigate rebellion. When
papers captured from rebels after a skirmish proved that
Warwick planned to place Clarence on the throne, Edward
took immediate action. Warwick and Clarence were proclaimed traitors and John Neville, the only member of his
family who had remained loyal to the king, was deprived of
the earldom of Northumberland. The title of Earl of Northumberland was restored to Henry Percy, a Lancastrian sym-
pathizer. [31] This was a rash action on Edward's part, and
one for which Richard would pay dearly.

Richard, who had been in Wales when the rebellion
started, set out with an army to aid his brother. Warwick
and Clarence, realizing full well that they would not win
against the combined armies of Richard of Gloucester and
the king, gathered together their wives, Warwick's younger
daughter Anne, and several hundred adherents, and fled to
the protection of Louis XI of France. [32]

King Edward, who knew his brother George and cousin Warwick well, realized that they would not give up the
fight so easily and he began preparations for the defense of
his kingdom. He sent Richard to the Midlands to raise
levies and maintain order. At the same time the king deprived the Nevilles of the Wardenship of the West Marches
and conferred the office on Richard, who he felt confident
could ensure the loyalty of Yorkshire. [33]

Meanwhile, Warwick had not been idle. Through the
mediation of his patron, Louis of France, the "Universal
Spider," Warwick had become reconciled with Margaret of
Anjou. In return for Warwick's promise to restore Henry
VI to the throne, Margaret had consented to the marriage of
her son Edward to Warwick's daughter, Anne Neville. The
marriage was not to be solemnized, however, until Warwick
had fulfilled his part of the agreement. [34] Clarence, who
had gained nothing by this agreement, was offered a consola-

tion prize. He was to inherit the throne if Anne and Edward
produced no heirs.

On September 13, 1470, Warwick landed in England
where he was joined by his brother, the Marquis of Montagu,
formerly the Earl of Northumberland. When Edward learned
of Montagu's defection, he and some of his followers, including Richard, Hastings, and Rivers fled to Burgundy. [35]
They took with them only the clothes on their backs and thus,
for the second time in his life, Richard found himself de-
pendent on the charity of the Duke of Burgundy. Charles the
Bold, the son of Philip the Good, was the husband of Edward and Richard's sister, Margaret. Charles, a descendant
of John of Gaunt, was at heart a Lancastrian. Political necessity, however, had turned him into a Yorkist. He was at
war with Louis XI and he knew that a Lancastrian king of
England would not lift a hand to help him. He must, therefore, give Edward the aid he needed to regain his throne.

Although Warwick had made good his promise to restore Henry to the throne, Margaret remained in France
with her son and Anne Neville, until she could be sure that
England was once more safely Lancastrian. Yorkist hopes
had been kept alive, on the other hand, by the birth of a son
to Elizabeth Woodville, who was then in sanctuary at Westminster. [36]

In March 1471 Edward returned to England. He met
with no resistance as he marched toward London, possibly
because he declared that he had come only to reclaim his
dukedom. [37] As he neared the city, however, he dropped
this pretense and many loyal Yorkists joined his ranks.
Even George of Clarence, either out of pique at Warwick or
a belated sense of family loyalty, came over to his brother's
side with the army he had raised to fight him. [38] London
welcomed Edward and supplied his army. A few days later
the king marched out of London to meet the kingmaker in
battle. With the Yorkist army rode the erstwhile king, Henry VI. [39]

On Easter Sunday, April 14, 1471, at the Battle of
Barnet, Warwick's army was annihilated and he and his
brother Montagu were slain. [40] The nineteen-year-old
Richard of Gloucester commanded the right wing of his
brother's victorious army. Three weeks later the royal
forces, with Richard in command of the left wing, crushed
the Lancastrians once and for all. On May 4, at Tewkes-

bury, Margaret's army was totally destroyed and her son
Edward lay among the dead.[41]

On May 21 the king entered London in a triumphal
procession led by his brother Richard. Accompanying the
royal train were Edward's prisoner, Margaret of Anjou, and
Clarence's ward, Anne Neville. That evening, according to
the official version, Henry VI died in the Tower of "pure
displeasure and melancholy."[42] There is no doubt that his
death was a judicial murder ordered by the king. The destruction of the legitimate Lancastrian line enabled Edward
IV to enjoy comparative peace for the rest of his reign.

In the months after Tewkesbury the grateful king
heaped yet more honors upon his youngest brother. Richard,
restored to his positions as Constable and Admiral of England, was also given Warwick's former office of Great Chamberlain and was made Steward of the Duchy of Lancaster beyond Trent. Because Richard had great affection for the
north country and the king needed a man of proven military
ability to deal with the constant troubles on the Scottish border, Richard fell heir to all of the estates and power in that
region that had formerly belonged to Warwick. Included in
the gift were the castles of Middleham and Sheriff Hutton.
The Duke of Gloucester thus became the greatest magnate in
the north, with authority over the Earl of Northumberland.[43]

Before leaving for the north to wage a campaign
against the Scots, Richard secured the king's permission to
marry Anne Neville. There had been a deep affection between the two young people since their childhood days at
Middleham and since Anne's betrothed, Edward of Lancaster,
was now dead, she was free to marry Richard. Upon the
successful completion of the Scottish campaign he returned
to London to claim his bride. Anne was in the custody of
her brother-in-law Clarence who had no intention of sharing
the Warwick inheritance with Richard. He therefore refused
to give up his charge, despite a warning from the king not
to interfere between the lovers. He claimed, when pressed,
that Anne had disappeared and that he neither knew nor cared
where she had gone. After weeks of diligent search Gloucester finally discovered Anne working as a kitchen maid in the
home of a retainer of the Duke of Clarence. Richard took
her at once to the sanctuary of St. Martin le Grande where
she would be safe from Clarence and from Richard too, if she
so desired.[44]

For several months the king's two brothers engaged
in a bitter dispute over the questions of the Warwick inheritance and Anne's guardianship. Richard was quite willing to
accept Anne even without her inheritance and so the matter
was finally settled. Richard was to keep Middleham and certain other of Warwick's Yorkshire estates and Clarence was
to get the rest of the vast inheritance.[45]

As soon as the property settlement had been reached,
Anne Neville came out of sanctuary. Without waiting for the
papal dispensation usual in marriages within this degree of
consanguinity,* Anne and Richard were married in the spring
of 1472, and they returned immediately to their childhood
home of Middleham.[46] There, in 1473, Anne was delivered
of their only child, Edward.

Following his marriage Richard extended his protection to other members of the Neville family. His mother-in-
law, stripped of her lands by her husband's attainder, came
out of sanctuary at Beaulieu Abbey and went to live in a
home which Richard provided for her. He helped to secure
the release of George Neville who had been imprisoned for
conspiracy and provided an annuity for Warwick's sister, the
Countess of Oxford, despite the fact that her husband was
actively working to overthrow the Yorkist king.[47]

In answer to the king's summons, Richard returned
to London in the spring of 1475. Edward had decided to in-
vade France, reconquer the territories lost by Henry VI,
and make good the English claim to the French throne.[48]
The money for the venture was raised by benevolence, the
army by indentures.[49] The Dukes of Clarence and Gloucester were each ordered to bring into the field one hundred
and twenty men-at-arms and one thousand archers. So
eager were the men of Yorkshire to wear Richard's badge
of the White / Boar that he was able to enlist at least three
hundred more men than he had contracted for.[50]

The invasion was a fiasco. Edward's allies deserted
him and he was forced to accept the French king's offer of
peace. This decision, although favored by most of the English councillors who had been handsomely bribed by Louis,
was bitterly opposed by the Duke of Gloucester. He saw

---

*Richard's mother and Warwick's father were brother and
sister, thus Richard and Warwick were first cousins, and
Richard and Anne were first cousins, once removed.

the Treaty of Péquigny, under which Edward was to receive
a large French annuity for life, as a humiliating defeat for
England. Richard was the only member of the royal party
to refuse the French king's bribe, [51] which increased his
popularity in England but earned him the undying enmity of
France.

Upon his return to England, Richard retired once more
to Yorkshire. Early in 1477 Edward summoned him to London to discuss the crisis which had arisen with the death of
Duke Charles of Burgundy. Clarence, a recent widower, suggested that he be permitted to marry Charles's heir, Mary,
in order to protect the English interest in Burgundy. Edward, however, did not intend to see his shallow, ambitious
brother become the ruler of the richest duchy in Europe,
and so he refused to allow the marriage. [52] Clarence reacted to this snub with almost insane fury. He arrested and
executed two of his late wife's servants on false charges,
armed his retainers, and publicly accused the king of trying
to destroy him. [53] For years Edward had endured with remarkable restraint Clarence's ambition, disloyalty, and even
his treason, but this time his unstable brother had gone a
step too far. In order to bolster his own claim to the throne,
Clarence had spread the story that Edward was the offspring
of an adulterous union between the Duchess of York and an
unknown archer. If this were not enough, he cast doubt as
well on the validity of Edward's marriage to Elizabeth Woodville. [54]

Richard, who had returned to Yorkshire early in the
year, hastened back to London when he learned that Clarence
had been arrested, charged with treason, and sent to the
Tower. He pleaded with Edward to spare Clarence's life,
but the Woodvilles, pressing from the other side, persuaded
the king not to yield. [55]

On January 16, 1478, parliament met to try Clarence
on the charge of high treason. Edward was the sole ac-
cusor and only Clarence spoke in his own defense. On
February 7 the High Steward passed the death sentence but
Edward vacillated until, on February 18, the Speaker of the
Commons petitioned the Lords to carry out the sentence. [56]
That same day Clarence was executed, by drowning, according to the story current at the time, in a butt of his favorite
malmsey wine. [57] Richard did not profit from his brother's
death. He merely regained the office of Great Chamberlain
which he had given up to Clarence fifteen years earlier, and

Richard's son Edward was given the title and dignity of Earl
of Salisbury. [58]

   Throughout these turbulent years Richard had spent
most of his time in the north, traditionally the unruliest
part of the kingdom, and he had succeeded in making himself popular by his wise and firm rule. He returned there
immediately after Clarence's execution and in the next four
years he visited London only twice--once in 1480 to see his
sister Margaret who had come from Burgundy to visit her
family, and again in 1481 to advise the king about the war
with Scotland. At Middleham he led the life typical of a
rich and powerful country lord. He delegated much of the
judicial work connected with his two most important national
offices, Constable and Admiral of England, to experienced
judges, but he held many lesser offices as well. None kept
him busier than the position of Warden of the West Marches,
which included supervisory authority over the East and Middle Marches under the Wardenship of the Earl of Northumberland. Despite the truce with the Scots, there were frequent
armed attacks from across the border and Richard spent much
of his time seeing to it that the frontier fortresses were
garrisoned, provisioned, and repaired. He established a
standard of excellence for the Warden of the Marches which
his successors found difficult to maintain. [59]

   The Council for the Marches, the Warden's advisory
body, acted also as a court of appeal for poor tenants who
were otherwise at the mercy of powerful lords. Any man,
from the lowliest peasant to the greatest lord, could ask and
receive justice from the Warden and his Council. In order
to maintain a harmonious relationship with Henry Percy,
Earl of Northumberland, whose family had previously been
lords of the North, Richard used him as an assistant in
judicial cases and in the affairs of the City of York, as well
as appointing him second-in-command in the wars against the
Scots. Percy, however, was no more satisfied with second
best than Clarence had been, and he never became a devoted
adherent of the Duke of Gloucester.

   Richard was never too busy to attend to problems
brought to his attention by the citizens of York, and his concern for their welfare earned him their wholehearted devotion. He was asked to settle important questions, such as
disputed elections, as well as lesser problems such as ordering the removal of the fishgarths which impeded transporta-
tion and reduced the number of fish the poor were able to

catch. [60]   Richard's interest in and support of the city was
deeply appreciated by the citizens who remained his faithful
and outspoken adherents well into the Tudor period.

In 1482, after years of unproductive and halfhearted
attempts to settle the Scottish problem, the king decided on
war as the final solution.   Edward's health, which had de-
teriorated after years of dissipation and riotous living, prevented him from taking an active role in the fighting, and
Richard was given complete charge of the campaign. [61]   He
regained Berwick-on-Tweed which had been ceded to Scotland
years before by Margaret of Anjou, and he captured Edin-
burgh without the loss of a single man.   The Scots thereupon
sued for peace, and Richard returned in triumph to London
in January 1483 for the opening of parliament.   He was wild-
ly acclaimed for the success of the campaign. [62]

The parliament showed its gratitude to Richard in a
tangible way by granting him what was, in effect, a practical-
ly autonomous palatinate in Cumberland County and the Scots
Marches.   The grants included the permanent Wardenship of
the West Marches and many lands, manors, and perquisites. [63]

The change which Richard found in his brother during
this visit left him profoundly disturbed.   Edward had grown
fat and lazy and he seemed to live only for pleasure.   Richard, whose outlook on life was puritanical compared to Edward's, no doubt blamed the influence of the loose-living
Woodvilles and Lord Hastings for his brother's decline.   He
had no way of knowing when he left London to return home
in February 1483 that he would never see his brother again.

Three

THE SHORT REIGN OF RICHARD III

Uneasy lies the head that wears a crown.
--<u>King Henry IV, Pt II</u>. 111.i.

On April 9, 1483, three weeks before his 41st birth-
day, Edward IV died.[1] A day or two prior to his death he
had added a codicil to his will naming his brother Richard
Protector and Defensor of the Realm and giving into his care
his young son, soon to be King Edward V.[2] Before his
death Edward had sought to reconcile the warring factions in
his court. He realized that when he was gone each side
would attempt to gain control of the young king, and a civil
war could well be the result. Therefore, in a dramatic
deathbed scene, he asked Lord Hastings and the queen's son,
the Marquis of Dorset, to clasp hands and swear love and
friendship to each other.[3] The reconciliation remained in
effect until the king drew his last breath.

Richard, who was at Middleham, did not learn of his
brother's death for nearly a week. Even then, the news
came, not from the queen or the council, but in a frantic
note from Hastings, the Lord Chamberlain, who informed
Richard of his appointment as Protector and urged him to
secure the person of the young king and come to London with
an armed escort as soon as possible.[4]

The new king, the twelve-year-old Edward, had been
living for many years at Ludlow Castle on the Welsh Marches
under the care of his maternal uncle Anthony Woodville, Earl
Rivers. There he ruled through a council whose titular head
was the Bishop of Worcester but which was dominated by the
Woodvilles and their adherents.

As soon as Richard learned of his brother's death,
he wrote to Rivers to inquire when, and by what route, the
young king would be brought to London, in order that they

might meet and enter the city together. Richard waited in vain for official notification from London of his brother's death and his own appointment as Protector. Nevertheless, he wrote to the queen to express his condolences and to pledge his loyalty to the new king. Alarmed by a second letter from Hastings, which informed him that, contrary to custom, the Woodvilles were taking over the government and had with difficulty been persuaded to confine the king's escort to two thousand armed men, Richard wrote to the council. [5] He reminded the members that according to law, custom, and his brother's will, he was Protector of the Realm and cautioned that no action could be taken in council contrary to any of these. [6] The law to which Richard referred would today be called "recognized precedent" since no laws of the time governed either the succession or the formation of a regency. [7] This council itself was, strictly speaking, no longer a legal body since the king's council, made up of advisors appointed by him, died with the king, just as parliament did. This did not, however, prevent the queen from attempting to use the council to seize power for herself and her family.

Shortly after Richard had written to the queen and the council, he received a letter from the Duke of Buckingham who was then in residence at his castle at Brecon in South Wales. Buckingham offered the Protector his support and the service of one thousand armed men. Richard accepted the offer of support, but asked the duke to bring only three hundred men, the same number he, himself, planned to bring. [8]

Before starting on his journey south, Richard personally administered to all his retainers and the magistrates of the City of York, an oath of allegiance to the new king. [9] On April 20 he set out with his party. It was arranged that he and Buckingham would meet Rivers and the king at Northampton on April 29.

The news which Richard received en route was not reassuring. Hastings reported from London that the queen's faction, ignoring Richard's appointment as Protector, had gone ahead with plans for an immediate coronation. [10] Once the king was crowned a Protector would, of course, be unnecessary, and the Woodvilles could rule through the child king.

The Woodvilles were taking a desperate gamble in

order to hold on to power.   They were hated by the old nobility and the commons for their greed and arrogance and,
unless they were able to retain their hold over the new king,
they could not hope to survive.   To do this they must, at all
costs, prevent the Protectorship under Richard of Gloucester.

The Woodvilles' maneuvers to maintain their position
had begun as soon it became apparent that Edward IV was
dying.   They were strongly entrenched in the council, for it
included among its members the Marquis of Dorset, the
queen's elder son by her first marriage, and three of her
brothers--Lionel, Bishop of Salisbury, Sir Edward Woodville,
and Anthony, Earl Rivers.   In addition, members of the up-
per clergy whom Edward had protected against a rising tide
of anti-clericalism which had swept the country, could be
counted on for support.   Moreover, Dorset, as Constable of
the Tower, controlled both the treasure and the armaments
of the kingdom, and Rivers controlled the young king. [11]

The queen's first move in the power struggle was
taken while Richard was en route to Northampton.   She
called the council together and secured approval for a proposal that a fleet be put together under the command of Sir
Edward Woodville, ostensibly for the purpose of fighting off
French privateers who were harrying English shipping. [12]
Without waiting for permission from the council, Dorset gave
his uncle, Sir Edward, part of the royal treasure and divided
the rest between himself and his mother.   He and the queen
then appointed a commission, made up of members of the
family and their adherents, to collect the tax which had been
levied by the last parliament. [13]   All of these actions were
illegal, but Dorset finally overreached himself when he pro-
posed that the coronation be held on May 4. [14]   Had the
Woodvilles succeeded in their attempt to have the coronation
over and done with before the Protector reached London they
would have been firmly entrenched in power, for the king,
the Tower, the treasure, the fleet, and the council--in short,
the whole apparatus of the government--would have been se-
curely in their hands.

The queen's next move encountered some resistance
from the council, for many of the members were becoming
thoroughly alarmed by the actions of the Woodvilles.   When
the council attempted to define the powers of the Protector,
the queen's faction claimed that the title carried with it no
more than first place on the council and even that position
was to last only until the coronation.   Some members, how-

ever, reminded the queen that the council itself had no power at all to decide the matter.   It was at this point that
Richard's letter reached the council and it served to gain
him the support of all except those committed to the Woodvilles.   Dorset openly asserted that if Richard gained ascend-
ency over the king, neither the Woodvilles nor their friends
would be safe.   As a result, the council voted to deprive the
Protector of any power.   Dorset thereupon wrote confidently
to Earl Rivers instructing him to be sure that he and the
king reached London by May 1. [15]

When Richard arrived at Northampton on April 29, the
king had already passed through the town and was lodged at
Stony Stratford, fourteen miles further along the road to London.   Rivers assured Richard that the move had been necessary because Northampton had insufficient accommodations
for the party.   Rivers, however, planned to stay the night
in Northampton and, when later that same day Buckingham
arrived, the three noblemen spent a seemingly friendly evening together.   The hour was late when Rivers retired to his
inn and, when he had gone, Richard and Buckingham discussed their plans.

The following morning Rivers awoke to find his inn
surrounded by armed men wearing Gloucester's badge of the
White Boar.   Guards had been posted along the road to
Stony Stratford to intercept any messages he might try to
send, and before Richard and Buckingham departed they
placed Rivers under arrest. [16]   When the two dukes reached
Stony Stratford the king and his escort were mounted and
ready to leave.   At the king's side were an old retainer,
Sir Thomas Vaughn, and Lord Richard Grey, the queen's
younger son by her first marriage.   Richard ordered the
arrest of Grey and Vaughn and excused his action to the
angry and astonished young king, explaining that these two,
and others of the queen-mother's faction, had hastened his
father's death by encouraging him in his excesses, thus
ruining his health.   He also charged that they had plotted to
circumvent Edward IV's will by depriving Richard, first of
the Protectorship, and ultimately of his life. [17]   Thereupon,
Richard dismissed the king's escort and conducted his nephew back to Northampton.   All of the king's Woodville attend-
ants were replaced by men loyal to the Protector, following
which Richard sent an explanation of his actions to the Lords
and the magistrates of London.   Woodville adherents also
raced to London with the news of what had happened to their
well-laid plans. [18]

When Dorset learned of the events at Northampton, he tried desperately but unsuccessfully, to rally the support of the Lords to raise a force to take the young king away from the Protector. When this attempt failed, he, his mother, her brother Lionel, Bishop of Salisbury, her five young daughters, and her son Richard, Duke of York, went hastily to the sanctuary of Westminster Abbey.[19] They took with them not only their share of the treasure but much of the late king's furniture, plate, jewels, and tapestries. The queen was in such a panic to save her possessions that she ordered a wall in the sanctuary broken through in order to get them in more quickly.[20]

The council voiced approval of the actions Richard had taken in regard to the young king, and on May 4, the royal party entered London to be greeted with great enthusiasm by the mayor, aldermen, and thousands of cheering citizens. The king was conducted to the palace of the Bishop of London where the Lords were assembled to pay him homage, and Richard went to Crosby's Place, his London home. Thus ended the day which the Woodvilles had chosen for the coronation of Edward V.

Richard's first task was to restore orderly government. He called a council which included many Woodville adherents. It was, in fact, composed of substantially the same membership as the one which had preceded it. The new council, acting in accordance with the late king's will, proclaimed Richard Protector and Defensor of the Realm.[21] Richard, in turn, promised to be guided by council decisions. At the suggestion of Buckingham, the council decided to move the king to the royal apartments in the Tower and set June 24 as the coronation day.[22] Summonses were sent for a parliament to convene on the day following the coronation. The council also agreed to propose to parliament that the Protectorship be continued until the king came of age in order to forestall the formation of factions which might seek to control the young king.[23]

One of Richard's first acts as Protector was to offer a pardon to all soldiers and sailors who would desert Edward Woodville and proclaim their loyalty to the new regime. Most of them accepted the offer, but Woodville himself escaped to Brittany with a large share of the treasure. This money was eventually turned over to Henry Tudor and it helped to finance his invasion in 1485.[24]

Buckingham quickly emerged as one of the most powerful and influential members of the council, overshadowing
men such as Hastings and Stanley who had served under Edward IV. His rapid elevation to power caused jealousy which
in turn led to intrigue between Hastings and the Woodvilles
and, eventually, to Hastings' death. Richard, of course,
appreciated Buckingham's loyal support, but he may have been
first drawn to him by the resemblance to George of Clarence,
Richard's late brother. Another mark in Buckingham's favor
was the fact that he had come to court in the new reign and
was, therefore, uninvolved in the entanglements and intrigues
of the late reign. Richard was, no doubt, aware that Buckingham's bitter hatred of the Woodvilles, caused by his
forced marriage to Katherine Woodville in his early adoles-
cence, was a prime factor in his decision to join ranks with
the Protector. Whatever the reasons, for the next few
months Buckingham was Richard's most ardent and outspoken
supporter. "He created, he was, the party of the Protector."[25]

Richard's fear that factions might form within the
council proved well-founded. To counter Buckingham's
rising influence, Hastings and his friends, including Rotherham, Morton, and Stanley, began meeting secretly and in-
triguing with the queen, using as their go-between Jane
Shore, the mistress of the late king and more recently of
Hastings and Dorset. Apparently they planned to end the
Protectorship and restore the Woodvilles to power.[26] Had
they succeeded, the Hastings-Woodville faction would have
been able to rule through the young king, and the position,
possibly even the life, of the Protector would have been in
jeopardy.

Richard was aware of what was going on and the danger the conspirators presented to his position. On June 10,
he wrote to the magistrates of York asking them to send as
many armed men as they could spare to assist him against
"the Queen, her blood adherents, and affinity, which have
intended, and daily doth intend, to murder and utterly destroy us and our cousin the duke of Buckingham, and the old
royal blood of this realm."[27] The city sent three hundred
men, who did not reach London, however, until after Richard's coronation.

On June 13, the council met in the Tower. Richard
opened the meeting with the announcement that a conspiracy
against the government had been discovered. He accused

the queen and her followers, including Jane Shore, Stanley,
Morton, Rotherham, and Hastings of complicity in the plot.
Hastings denied the charge, but the four men were arrested
and Hastings was taken at once to the Tower green and sum-
marily executed. [28]

A herald was sent through the city to read a proclamation justifying the Protector's action. Hastings, Richard
charged, had been involved in a plot against the Protector
and Buckingham, and his immediate execution was necessary
in order to prevent any attempt to rescue him. It seems
remarkable that the execution, without a trial, of a man as
popular as Hastings raised no protest among the citizens.
It is quite likely, however, that many Londoners were already convinced that Richard intended to take the crown. [29]

Richard took Hastings' widow under his protection and
permitted her to keep all of her husband's property. Possibly this was Richard's way of atoning for an act he may have
deeply regretted. [30] Stanley and Rotherham, however, were
imprisoned only briefly, and were later restored to the
council. At Buckingham's request, Morton was placed in
his charge and sent to Brecon Castle in Wales. On June
25, at Pontefract, Rivers, Grey, and Vaughn were executed
for treason, thus ending, Richard hoped, all danger of further Woodville intrigue. [31]

Most of the council members had supported Richard's
actions with regard to Hastings and the other conspirators,
and they now acceded to his request that Elizabeth Woodville
and her children be asked to leave sanctuary. Even if she
refused, her younger son was to be brought out to join his
brother and to attend the coronation. The council agreed
with Buckingham, who argued that since the children had
done no wrong they had no need of sanctuary. On June 16,
a delegation from the council, headed by the Archbishop of
Canterbury, went to Westminster and persuaded the reluctant
queen to give up her son. Prince Richard thereupon joined
his brother in the Tower. [32]

In London, where the council had again postponed the
coronation, there were rumors that Edward V would lose his
crown before long. The reason for the postponement was
the startling news, imparted to Richard and some members
of the council by Bishop Stillington of Bath and Wells, to the
effect that prior to the Woodville marriage the late king had
made a pre-contract of marriage with Dame Eleanor Butler,

daughter of the Earl of Shrewesbury. [33] If true, this made
the Woodville marriage invalid in the eyes of the church and
made the children of the marriage illegitimate. Although
such pre-contracts were frequently set aside, and it is unknown what, if any, evidence Stillington produced to prove
his claim, Richard accepted the story. The history of
Clarence's trial and execution, and Stillington's subsequent
arrest, have led several historians to suggest that Clarence
knew the secret and was put to death at the insistence of the
Woodvilles in order to protect their position. [34]

On Sunday, June 22, at Paul's Cross, Friar Ralph
Shaa, the brother of the Mayor of London, preached a sermon, taking for his text, "Bastard slips shall not take root."
He told the congregation of the pre-contract and declared the
Duke of Gloucester to be the true heir to the throne. In
other parts of the city other preachers, acting on instructions from the Duke of Buckingham, even went so far as to
impugn the legitimacy of Edward IV himself. This scandal-
ous accusation had been levied years before by Clarence
when he had aimed at the throne, but there is no evidence
to show that Richard condoned this attack on his mother's
reputation. The fact that he moved into his mother's house
at this time rather tends to prove the opposite. [35]

On Monday following Dr. Shaa's sermon, the Duke of
Buckingham addressed the assembled Lords and on Tuesday
he spoke to the magistrates and chief citizens of London at
the Guildhall. The crown, he told both groups, belonged
rightfully to Richard of Gloucester. On Wednesday, June 25,
a parliament in fact, if not in name, met at Westminster
and drew up a petition in which they reviewed the charges
relating to the pre-contract and the illegitimacy of Edward's
children and implored Richard to take the throne. Their petition was unanimously approved and was formally presented
to Richard at Baynard's Castle on the following day. After
a show of reluctance, he accepted the petition and the crown.
The whole assembly then repaired to Westminster where
Richard seated himself on the marble chair of the King's
Bench and, on that day, he began his reign. On July 6, in
a magnificent ceremony, Richard and Anne were crowned in
Westminster Abbey, with virtually every peer and leading
citizen in attendance. [36]

Two weeks after the coronation the new king and
queen set out on progress throughout the kingdom, accompanied by many bishops, lords, judges, and household offi-

cials, but no armed men. At Gloucester, they were joined
by Buckingham, who had remained in London and was now
on his way to Brecon. It was to be the last meeting between
the king and his chief supporter. [37]

When Richard reached Lincoln early in October he
learned, to his great surprise and dismay, that Buckingham
had revolted against him. The uprising had begun in the
southern and southwestern counties as a Lancastrian and
Woodville attempt to put Edward V back on the throne. By
the time Buckingham reached Brecon, plans for the rebellion
had already been laid. Apprised of the plot, and flattered
by the astute Bishop Morton, the duke quickly became involved in the treason. [38] It is quite possible that Morton
may have convinced Buckingham, who was descended from
Thomas of Woodstock, the youngest son of Edward III, that
he had a chance to claim the throne for himself. On the
other hand, Morton may have persuaded Buckingham to play
the king-maker once more by supporting the claim of Henry
Tudor. If Morton adopted the latter course, he no doubt argued persuasively that Tudor's chances of winning the crown
were greater than Buckingham's since Henry's mother had
great Lancastrian support and his promise to marry Elizabeth of York would gain him the aid and friendship of the
Woodvilles and many disaffected Yorkists. [39]

For reasons known only to himself, Buckingham agreed
to lend his support to Tudor's cause. The leaders of the revolt already in progress were informed that they could count
on the help of Buckingham and his large band of armed retainers. Within days, however, Buckingham and Morton
were able to turn the focus of the rebellion from Edward V
to Henry Tudor by informing the rebels that both the erstwhile young king and his brother had been put to death in an
unknown manner. [40] Whether the two boys were indeed dead
at this time is a point of much debate.

On October 15 Richard issued a proclamation declaring Buckingham a traitor and instructing his subjects to take
up arms against him. The proclamation forbade any man to
injure the person or possessions of any of Buckingham's followers who remained loyal to the king. This worked to the
advantage of Lord Stanley, whose wife, the mother of Henry
Tudor, was deeply involved in the rebellion, but who chose
at this time to remain personally loyal to the king. [41] It
was fortunate for Stanley that he did, for the rebellion was
a disaster from the moment Buckingham assumed leadership

of it. Buckingham's troops, many of whom had been forced
to join his army against their will, deserted in large numbers. [42] He was attacked during the march through Wales by
bands of men loyal to the king.   It was the weather, however, which proved his undoing.   A great storm, known to
this day as Buckingham's Great Water, arose and washed
out roads, bridges, and fields.   Morton, sensing that disaster impended, deserted the duke and fled to Flanders to
await a better opportunity. [43]

Buckingham, no doubt realizing that he had been used
and discarded by the bishop, donned rough work clothes and
fled to Shropshire where he sought refuge in the home of a
retainer.   The enormous price on Buckingham's head put too
great a strain on the loyalty of his retainer and Buckingham
was turned over to agents of the king.   He was brought to
Salisbury where, hysterical with fear, he related all the details of the plot and begged for an interview with Richard.
His request was denied and on November 2, in the market
square, the would-be kingmaker was beheaded. [44]   When Henry Tudor, whose fleet was anchored off Plymouth, learned of
the fate of Buckingham and the rebellion, he returned to
France. [45]

Richard showed great clemency to most of the rebels.
Ten of the leaders were executed but many of the others
were pardoned.   Lady Stanley was deprived of her titles and
estates which were given to her husband and she herself was
placed in her lord's custody.   Both Stanley and Northumberland profited greatly from the confiscated estates of the Duke
of Buckingham. [46]

On January 23, 1484, two months after the collapse
of Buckingham's rebellion, Richard's only parliament con-
vened at Westminster.   Chancellor Russell delivered the opening address.   In addition to the Titulus Regis, which con-
firmed the act of the previous parliament settling the crown
on Richard, [47] this parliament passed several important
pieces of legislation.   Benevolences were made illegal and
the legal machinery of government was reformed in order to
protect the ordinary citizen.   These acts, passed at the request of the king and his council, earned for Richard the
support of the commons.   The nobility and gentry, who had
for years been using the law to overawe and prey on the
lower classes, were alienated by Richard's insistence on reform.   One interesting and probably noncontroversial act
passed in this reign strictly regulated the activities of for-

eign merchants in England. At Richard's request a clause
was inserted which exempted any foreigner engaged in the
printing, binding, or selling of books.   This was the first
piece of legislation in England which protected and fostered
the art of printing. [48]

Early in March 1484, after Richard had sworn publicly to protect and find suitable husbands for them, the five
daughters of Elizabeth Woodville came out of sanctuary. [49]
It is probable, though not certain, that Elizabeth joined them.
She was given a pension of seven hundred marks a year and
each of her daughters was provided with a small dowry.
Elizabeth wrote to her son Dorset, who was in Brittany,
telling him it was safe for him to return to England.   He
did, indeed, attempt to return but was captured by agents of
Henry Tudor and taken to Paris. [50]   Obviously at this time
the Woodvilles felt that they had nothing to fear from King
Richard.

In April 1484 the royal couple's only child, Edward,
Prince of Wales, died at Middleham Castle. [51]   Although he
had been sickly from birth, his death was a blow from which
his parents never fully recovered.   On August 21, Richard
appointed his nephew, John de la Pole, Earl of Lincoln, as
Lieutenant of Ireland, a position traditionally given by the
Yorkist kings to the heir apparent. [52]

On March 11, 1485, Anne Neville died, probably of
tuberculosis.   Almost immediately rumors circulated to the
effect that the king planned to marry his niece Elizabeth and
that he may have hurried his wife into her grave.   It is possible that some people believed that Richard would make
Elizabeth his wife in order to undercut Henry Tudor whose
bid for Yorkist support was based on his promise to marry
the young heiress.   At the urging of his councillors, Richard
appeared before the magistrates of London and the Lords and
firmly denied that there was any truth in the slander, charg-
ing that it was the work of Tudor's agents. [53]

Henry Tudor, encouraged by the promise of French
aid, had already begun serious preparations for his invasion.
Richard, realizing the gravity of the situation, made plans
for the defense of his realm.   He sent a fleet to guard the
Channel and reinforced the defenses of the towns.   Commis-
sions of Array were sent to all the counties. [54]

Lord Stanley, stepfather to Henry Tudor, now began

his maneuvers, designed to assure his place on the winning
side, whichever it turned out to be. He asked the king's
permission to return to his estates so that he would be in a
better position to raise support for the king in case of an invasion. The Stanleys had a long history of treason to both
Lancaster and York but had always managed not only to avoid
the usual consequences of treason but also to reap great re-
wards in the bargain. Richard, who was well aware of Stanley's record and character, agreed to the request. To con-
ciliate his councillors, however, he sent for Stanley's son,
Lord Strange, to act as his father's deputy and as surety for
his father's loyalty. [55]

On Sunday, August 7, 1485, Henry Tudor landed with
his army at Milford Haven in South Wales. [56] His soldiers
were, for the great part, criminals released from the jails
of Normandy on the condition that they accompany Tudor to
England. [57] Their generals were Henry's uncle, Jasper Tudor, the Lancastrian Earl of Pembroke, and John, Earl of
Oxford. Henry Tudor had never fought a battle in his life. [58]

Tudor, who had chosen for his banner the red dragon
of Cadwallader, picked up some support from the Welsh who
saw him as a new King Arthur come to claim his and their
rightful place as rulers of England. He won the support of
the leading chieftain of Wales, Rhys ap Thomas, by promising him the lieutenantship of Wales for life. [59] This greatly strengthened his cause, but his hopes of a general uprising in his favor proved to be unfounded.

When Richard learned of the invasion, he instructed
his captains to join him at Leicester. Lord Stanley, upon
being ordered to meet the king at Nottingham, sent word
that he was suffering from the sweating sickness and was
therefore unable to obey the summons. Lord Strange, captured during an attempted escape, admitted that his uncle,
Sir William Stanley, planned to betray the king. He insist-
ed, however, that his father intended no treason, and wrote
to Lord Stanley begging him to join the king with his retainers. [60]

The Stanleys were not Richard's only source of wor-
ry. He learned that the Earl of Northumberland, the Commissioner of Array for the East Riding, had failed to sum-
mon the men of York, possibly because he resented their
loyalty to Richard. When the magistrates of York were
apprised of the situation, they sent eighty men to aid the
king. [61]

On August 19, having learned that Tudor's army was marching toward Leicester, Richard turned south from Nottingham with his forces.   He was joined by the Duke of Norfolk, but the Earl of Northumberland and his army lagged behind.   To the west lay the armies of the Stanleys, and bringing up the rear was the rag-tag collection of French criminals and Welshmen marching under the banner of Henry Tudor.   En route, a secret meeting took place at Atherstone, during which the Stanleys promised Henry Tudor that they would aid him in the coming battle, throwing in their forces when they felt the time was right.   Henry fully realized, however, that if Richard's army seemed to be winning, the Stanleys would not hesitate to support the king.   He never forgave them for their equivocation. [62]

Late in the day of August 20, Northumberland and his army reached Leicester.   His men, he told Richard, were exhausted after their long march and would do better service in the rear, rather than in the thick of the fighting.   Richard no doubt knew that he could not count on Percy.   All his life Percy had resented the power Richard held over the men of the north--power that had been exercised by the Percy family for generations and which they felt was rightfully theirs.   Indeed, it is quite probable that Percy had already secured a pardon from Henry Tudor in the hope that Henry would be victorious and would, in return for such support, restore the Percies to a position of power in the north. [63]

On August 22, on Redmore Plain a few miles outside the little town of Market Bosworth, the king addressed his troops.   His sleep had been disturbed by dreams, and those around him noted that he was paler than usual.   No matter who won the field that day, he told his men, the England that they knew would be destroyed.   If Tudor won, he would crush the supporters of the House of York and rule by fear. If Richard won, he too would rule by force since his attempts to win loyalty by fairness and kindness had failed. The absence of a chaplain to say mass before the battle was intentional, the king declared.   If their quarrel were God's, no prayers were needed; if not, their prayers were idle blasphemy. [64]

Richard then sent a last message to Lord Stanley, ordering him to join the royal army if he valued his son's life.   Stanley replied that he had other sons and for the present was not inclined to join the king.   In a burst of anger, Richard ordered the immediate execution of Strange, but thought better of it and decided instead to keep him under close guard. 65

As Richard prepared to go into battle some members of his household begged him not to wear the crown which would mark him out for destruction by the enemy. He replied that he would live and die King of England. Then, surrounded by his knights and esquires of the body, he rode out to join battle with the Welsh challenger. 66

Henry Tudor had probably five thousand men in the field, of which two thousand were French. Lord Stanley's force numbered between thirty-five hundred and four thousand, and his brother, Sir William, had about twenty-five hundred men under his command. Richard's army was about twice as large as Tudor's, but smaller than the combined Tudor-Stanley forces. Three thousand of Richard's nine thousand men were under the command of Northumberland and so took no part in the fighting. 67

In the midst of the battle, a messenger pointed out to Richard a figure on horseback, motionless on a hill. Above his head waved the banner of the red dragon of Cadwallader and surrounding him were about two hundred and fifty armed men. Quickly Richard decided to take the one desperate chance which must end in brilliant victory or disastrous defeat. 68 If he and the men of his household could cross in front of Sir William Stanley's much larger force, he would have a chance to reach Tudor and destroy him and his cause with one blow. The terrible news that Norfolk and Lord Ferrers had been killed reached Richard and he spied a messenger from Tudor, hurrying to inform Lord Stanley of their deaths. Northumberland refused to obey when the king ordered him to move in to support the royal forces and Richard knew that his only chance for survival lay in Tudor's death. 69

Rejecting Catesby's plea to flee while there was yet time, Richard and his household knights mounted their horses. Richard gripped his battle axe, signalled his trumpeters, and he and his men started slowly down the hill. At the bottom they broke into a gallop. Past the Stanley lines they rode, straight toward the ranks of the Tudor guards. Richard first encountered huge Sir John Cheney, felled him with his axe, and pushed on toward the pretender. Tudor recoiled from the sight of the slight, menacing figure slashing with his battle axe through the

guards. [70] Richard reached William Brandon, Henry's standard bearer, and struck him down.   Just as Richard and his
knights reached their target, the troops of Sir William Stanley bore down on them.   Part of the king's men turned to
meet the cavalry charge, and Richard and the rest of his
men pressed on toward Tudor.   Suddenly, his men began to
fall about him, hacked by the weapons of their enemies.
"Treason! Treason!" cried the king as he pressed on toward his rival.   With all his household knights dead or
wounded, he fought on until the blows of a dozen weapons
smashed and hacked at him through his armor and beat him
down to the ground. [71]

After the battle, according to legend, Sir William
Stanley retrieved Richard's golden crown from under a bram-
ble bush and placed it on the head of Henry Tudor.   Richard's naked body, crusted with blood from his many wounds
and with a felon's halter around the neck, was slung across
the back of a horse and taken to Leicester. [72] For two days
the body lay at the Grey Friars, exposed for all to see, until the friars finally received permission to bury it in an un-
marked grave.   Years later, Henry VII allotted the sum of
ten pounds and one shilling to raise a modest tomb for the
man he had displaced.   At the dissolution of the monasteries
in the reign of Henry VIII, Richard's tomb was destroyed
and his remains were thrown into the River Soar. [73]

There are the essential facts concerning the life and
reign of Richard III.   But a mere recounting of the facts
leaves several important questions unanswered.   What became of the princes in the Tower?   Were they murdered
and, if so, who was responsible for the crime?   Must Richard take, or share, responsibility for the deaths of Edward
of Lancaster, Henry VI, Clarence, and his wife Anne?
What sort of man was Richard, physically, emotionally, and
mentally?   Many different theories have been suggested to
answer each of these questions over the past five hundred
years.   Some of them show great imagination, and an equally
great ignorance of the facts.   In many cases, the answers
are based on the writers' own interpretation or selection of
the facts.   In the following chapters we shall see how, and
possibly why, many historians and authors attempted to resolve the questions concerning Richard III and his reign.

Four

THE EARLY HISTORIANS

God and your arms be praised, victorious friends!
The day is ours; the bloody dog is dead.
                              --King Richard III, V, iii.

Myths, cherished and sanctified by time and repetition, have comprised an important part of the history of all people in every age. The fifteenth century is no exception and indeed, the history of the second half of that century, which has been described as "a patchwork of legend and rumour mingled with, and all too often taken for, fact"[1] can serve as a classic example of the persistence of traditional beliefs. The sources upon which most of these histories have been based are a conglomeration of "biased opinion, wild rumour, meretricious propaganda, the foulest of slander as well as historical truth."[2] Despite the development during the past century of more critical methods of evaluating historical sources, as well as the discovery of hitherto unknown contemporary documents, the history of the Yorkist period is still being viewed, to a great extent, in the light of Tudor tradition. Despite ever increasing attacks on its validity, this so-called "Tudor Myth" has been accepted for nearly five centuries as historical fact. An examination of the sources, and the ways in which they were used, amplified, and occasionally distorted by succeeding generations of chroniclers, historians, playwrights, poets, and novelists, may help to explain the reputation of Richard III.

There are few contemporary narrative sources for the life and reign of Richard III, and those which have survived are of varying degrees of reliability. Each reflects the Lancastrian or Yorkist bias of its author or his informants and, in many cases, rumor or opinion is reported as fact. Despite their flaws, however, much can be learned from them about Richard.

31

Three English chronicles, written by men who participated in, or witnessed the events in England between 1469 and 1485, the period during which Richard played a significant part in the country's affairs, are of considerable importance. * The Historie of the Arrivall of King Edward IV. in England, and the Final Recovery of His Kingdomes from Henry VI., A.D. 1471, commonly referred to as the Fleetwood Manuscript, was written by a servant of Edward IV shortly after the events it describes. [3] The chronicle covers a period of eleven weeks, from March 2, 1471, to May 27, 1471, and gives what might be called the official Yorkist version of several important events.

Warkworth's Chronicle of King Edward IV was written by Dr. John Warkworth, master of St. Peter's College, Cambridge, as an addition to a copy of Caxton's Chronicle of the Brute, which the author presented to the college library in 1483. [4] This narrative, by a Lancastrian partisan, deals with the years 1461 to 1473.

The work which covers the longest period of time, beginning with the Battle of Ludlow in 1459 and ending with Richard's death at Bosworth, is the Third Continuation of the Croyland Chronicle. † The author of this Continuation was a doctor of canon law and a member of King Edward's council, and his account of the reigns of Edward IV and Edward V seems to be based on personal knowledge. [5] It is quite probable, however, that his record of the events of July 1483 through August 1485 was based on what he learned from one or more outside sources and that one of his informants may have been Richard's chancellor, Bishop Russell. [6]

---

*The Chronicle of King Edward the Fourth, known as Hearne's Fragment, was written by a partisan of the House of York. It is not included with the three discussed above because unfortunately the portion of this Chronicle covering the period after 1470 has been lost. The surviving chapters are printed in The Chronicles of the White Rose of York, ed. by J. C. Giles (London: James Bohn, 1843).

†This continuation is referred to as the Second Continuation by C. L. Kingsford in English Historical Literature and P. M. Kendall in Richard III, but Henry T. Riley, editor and translator of Ingulph's Chronicle of the Abbey of Croyland, refers to it as the Third Continuation and this designation will be followed here.

Richard's reputation is based on the allegation that he was responsible for the murders of a great number of innocent people, among them his first two victims, Edward of Lancaster and Edward's father, Henry VI. Their deaths were, of course, of sufficient importance for each of these contemporary chroniclers to have recorded the circumstances under which they occurred. The author of the Arrivall, who was present at the Battle of Tewkesbury where Prince Edward met his death, merely states, "Edward, called Prince, was taken, fleinge to the towne wards, and slayne, in the fielde."[7] The Lancastrian Warkworth agrees that the prince was slain in the field, but adds that he "cryede for socoure to his brother-in-lawe the Duke of Clarence."[8] The Croyland continuator, who apparently did not witness the battle, declares Edward to have been slain "either on the field or after the battle, by the avenging hands of certain persons."[9]

These three contemporary writers show less unanimity in their reports of the death of King Henry, disagreeing on the date as well as the manner in which he met his end. The Yorkist version as given in the Arrivall is that when Henry learned of the death of his son and the destruction of the Lancastrian hopes at Tewkesbury, "he took it to so great despite, ire, and indignation, that of pure displeasure, and melancoly, he dyed the xxiij day of the monithe of May."[10] This chronicle further states that the royal party was not in London on the day of Henry's death, the king having come to the city on May 21,[11] where he remained for only one day.[12]

Warkworth's Chronicle tells a different story.

> And the same nyghte that Kynge Edwarde came to Londone, Kynge Herry, beynge inwarde in presone in the Toure of Londone, was putt to dethe the xxi. day of Maij, on a Tywesday nyght, b wix xi and xij of the cloke beynge thenne at the Toure the Duke of Gloucetre, brothere to Kynge Edwarde, and many other.[13]

According to the Croyland chronicler,

> Henry was found dead in the Tower of London; may God spare and grant time for repentence to the person, whoever he was, who thus dared to lay sacrilegious hands upon the Lord's anointed!

Hence it is that he who perpetrated this has justly
earned the title of tyrant. [14]

Many historians, including the translator of the Chronicle,
believe that the tyrant to whom the chronicler referred was
Edward IV. [15] Quite obviously, none of Richard's contemporaries believed that he was responsible for the death of
Prince Edward and only Warkworth, of the English chroniclers, hints at his complicity in Henry's murder.

Three Europeans of distinction recorded their impressions of certain aspects of English affairs during this period,
and each of these writers contributed one or two important
pieces of the picture.   It should be borne in mind, however,
that the views expressed in these works, if accepted uncrit-
ically, would present a distorted and incomplete story.

The Memoirs of Phillippe de Commynes is a work
usually cited as an important source of information about the
Yorkist period and, with certain significant reservations,
rightly so.   Commynes, a Burgundian nobleman, served as
councellor and chamberlain to Charles the Bold from 1464 until 1472, when he left to serve a new master, Charles's old
enemy, Louis XI of France. [16]   As the king's most trusted
advisor, he was at the center of affairs at the French court
until Louis's death in August 1483.   The Memoirs, which he
began in 1489 at the request of Angelo Cato, Archbishop of
Vienne, and completed in 1498, are valuable for accounts of
events which Commynes himself witnessed. [17] His reports
of what had occurred in England, however, were based on
information he received from Lancastrian exiles on the Continent prior to 1485, and from the Tudor version of the history of the period afterward. [18]

Angelo Cato, at whose request Commynes wrote his
Memoirs, was responsible for another significant history as
well.   Archbishop Cato, who planned to write a history of
the times of Louis XI, [19] sent an Italian cleric named Dominic Mancini to England in 1482 for the purpose of gathering
and reporting information about the country. [20]   Despite the
fact that Mancini probably knew no English, [21] had no understanding of English customs or institutions, [22] and quite possibly never laid eyes on Richard III, [23] he dutifully wrote his
impressions of the events in England between the death of
Edward IV, which he erroneously states as having occurred
on April 7, 1483, [24] and the coronation of Richard III.   His
chief informant was probably an English cleric named John
Argentine. [25]

Commynes occasionally expressed doubt about the accuracy of the information given him by his English acquaint-
ances. In describing the death of Henry VI, which he mistakenly places after the Battle of Barnet, he declares:

> If what I heard is not a lie, immediately after the
> battle, King Edward's brother, the duke of Glou-
> cester, who later became King Richard, killed this
> good man, King Henry, with his own hands, or had
> him taken to some secret place and had him killed
> while he looked on. [26]

As for Prince Edward, Commynes merely states that he was
"killed on the spot"[27] at the Battle of Tewkesbury. Mancini
does not mention either of these incidents.

Richard's next victim, according to the legend, was
his brother, George, Duke of Clarence, who died in the Tower in 1478. The Croyland chronicler, the only contemporary
writer resident in England at the time, relates the whole
sordid story but does not mention Richard's name in connection with Clarence's death, nor does he indicate the manner
in which the sentence was carried out. [28] Mancini places the
blame for Clarence's death on Elizabeth Woodville who, he
says, fearing that Clarence would deprive her son of the
crown, persuaded the king to destroy him. The unfortunate
duke met his end by being plunged into a jar of sweet wine. [29]
The Duke of Gloucester, according to Mancini, far from has-
tening his brother's death, was "so overcome with grief ...
that he was overheard to say that he would one day avenge
his brother's death. "[30]

The story of Clarence's drowning in a butt of sweet
wine, now specified as malmsey, is repeated by Commynes,
indicating that the rumor had become fairly widespread within a few years. [31] It was Clarence's desire for the throne,
Commynes declares, which prompted Edward to have him
put to death. [32]

The murders of Prince Edward, Henry VI, and Clarence which were recreated in scenes of poignant drama by
Shakespeare form the prelude of the saga. The central
theme, of course, is Richard's seizure of the crown which
was preceded by the executions of Rivers, Grey, and Hastings and followed by the murders of the two princes and, in
many versions of the story, of Richard's wife Anne. The
narratives written by the Croyland chronicler and Dominic

Mancini are the most detailed of all the accounts concerning
the period following the death of Edward IV.   Although he
was misinformed about certain facts of which he did not have
firsthand knowledge, [33] the Croyland chronicler was quite obviously in a position to describe many of the events from
personal experience.   His accounts of council meetings held
during the summer of 1483 could only have been written by
an eye-witness.   He relates that the "more prudent members
of the council" strongly opposed the appointment of any member of the queen's family as guardian of the young king. [34]
Nevertheless, he criticizes Richard for arresting Rivers and
Grey and for failing to show enough concern for preserving
the dignity and safety of the queen. [35]

        Most modern historians accept the chronology given
in the Croyland Chronicle for the death of Hastings on June
13 and the removal of the Duke of York from sanctuary on
June 16. [36]   Mancini, who omits the dates of both incidents,
reverses their chronology[37] and his version was accepted by
the Tudor historians.   Alison Hanham, a recent writer, contends, however, that it was the Croyland chronicler, rather
than Mancini and those who followed him, who was in error[38]
and that the Tudor writers were correct in believing that
Hastings, who opposed the planned usurpation, was removed
after Richard had both princes in his power. [39]   Hanham declares that Hastings was executed on June 20 and Richard
falsified the date on official documents in order to justify his
accusation that Hastings was involved in a treasonous plot.
Thus, this ingenious writer has managed, after nearly five
centuries, to uncover still another crime to heap on Richard's
bent, if not crooked, back.   The reversal of the chronology
and the falsification of the date of Hastings's death may have
been, she declares, "a deliberate manipulation of history in
his [Richard's] own interest. "[40]   One need hardly add that,
if that was the intention, it did not succeed.

        The Croyland chronicler, who was probably present at
the council meeting at which Hastings was arrested and executed, declares that the Chamberlain, Rotherham, and Morton were "removed without judgment or justice. "[41]   He is
similarly critical of the executions of Rivers and Grey which
took place ten days later. [42]   Mancini's version of these
events is substantially the san   as that of the Croyland continuator except that he mistakenly believed that Hastings was
killed in the Council room itself, by soldiers acting under
orders from the Duke of Buckingham. [43]

There are similarities as well as significant differ-
ences in the accounts of these contemporary writers of Richard's usurpation of the throne and the fate of the princes in
the Tower. The least detailed and most emphatic comes
from Commynes who, writing many years later, was merely
repeating rumors or opinions current at the time. Immediately after the death of Edward IV, Commynes declares,
Louis XI was notified and a few days later he received letters from Edward's younger brother who had already proclaimed himself king, and "who had had the two children of
his brother, King Edward, murdered ... and in a plenary
session of the parliament he had the two daughters of Edward
degraded and declared illegitimate."[44] Neither Richard nor
his partner in crime, Buckingham, whom Commynes also
implicates in the death of the princes, lived long to enjoy
the fruits of their crime.[45] Commynes, the cynical man of
the world who "could scarcely ever resist the pleasure of
drawing edifying and trite conclusions from the lessons of
history,"[46] saw in Richard's death at Bosworth "the judgment of God. But to make it more evident, as soon as King
Richard had his two nephews cruelly murdered, ... he lost
his wife. Some say that he had her slain. He had only one
son, who died soon after."[47]

Dominic Mancini, who wrote The Usurpation of Richard the Third before the end of 1483, seems to have made a
conscious effort to be objective and the work is relatively
free of the pious moralizing found throughout Commynes's
Memoirs. The narrative does, however, contain several
rather serious errors which have already been noted and
which were the result of the author's ignorance of English
language and customs, or the misinformation which he received from others. In addition, Mancini fails to date certain important events, among them Hasting's death[48] and
Richard's coronation,[49] and incorrectly dates others.[50]

Mancini's almost complete reliance on second-hand
reports and rumor for the materials of his history, quite
rightly deplored by most scholars, is of considerable value
in this particular instance. The rumors and opinions which
were current at this period have thus been preserved and
while they do not shed any light on the fate of the princes,
they do tend to show what some people thought about the
situation. Mancini learned from Dr. Argentine that after the
death of Hastings the two princes were withdrawn into inner
apartments of the Tower and eventually were seen no more.
Young Edward appears, according to the informant, to have

had a premonition of death and to have sought remission of
his sins through confession and penance. [51]   There seem to
have been some who believed, during the summer or fall of
1483, that at least the elder of the two boys was dead, for
Mancini declares:

> I have seen many men burst forth into tears and
> lamentations when mention was made of him after
> his removal from men's sight; and already there
> was a suspicion that he had been done away with....
> Whether, however, he has been done away with,
> and by what manner of death, so far I have not at
> all discovered. [52]

Indeed, neither Mancini nor anyone else ever discovered
whether, or by what manner the princes were done away
with, but in January 1484 the French Chancellor, in an address to the States-General, accused Richard III of murdering his nephews.   It is quite possible that Mancini was his
source[53] and not unlikely that the traditional French hatred
of the English was the motive for making this public accusation. [54]

Although Mancini seems to have assumed that Richard
planned to seize the throne immediately after Edward's
death, [55] he does not, like later Tudor writers, view Richard as an inhuman monster.   He praises Richard's administration in the north and attests that "the good reputation of
his private life and public activities powerfully attracted the
esteem of strangers. "[56]

The Croyland chronicler sheds no more light than does
Mancini on the mystery of the princes in the Tower.   He
tells of plots laid in the southern and western counties to release the princes from captivity.   A public proclamation was
made that Buckingham, who had repented of his former conduct, would lead the rebellion.   It was at this point, declares the chronicler, that "a rumour was spread that the
sons of the king Edward before-named had died a violent
death, but it was uncertain how. "[57]   It was then that the
Bishop of Ely, John Morton, persuaded Buckingham to offer
the throne to Henry Tudor if he would marry Elizabeth of
York. [58]

During the Christmas festivities of 1484, which the
Croyland chronicler considered remarkable for their splendor
and which he censured because "far too much attention was

given to dancing and gaiety, and vain changes of apparel presented to queen Anne and the lady Elizabeth,"[59] the similarity of these two ladies' gowns caused some comment. Some people were said to wonder if the king anticipated the queen's death, or planned to divorce her in order to marry his niece. When Anne died the following month, Richard publicly denied that he had ever intended to marry Elizabeth, a denial which, says the chronicler, not everyone believed.[60]

At Bosworth, declares the chronicler, heaven granted a glorious victory to the Earl of Richmond, while Richard "fell in the field like a brave and most valiant prince."[61] The treatment given the late king's corpse was "not exactly in accordance with the laws of humanity"[62] but it may have been an indication of what the surviving Plantagenets could expect from the new king.

Several errors of fact contained in the Croyland narrative have led more than one historian to the belief that two writers had a hand in compiling the work.[63] Paul Murray Kendall surmises that the first part of the Continuation was based on Bishop Russell's information, but that the bishop did not complete the account. A second writer, possibly the prior of the abbey, "supplied the inaccurate and distorted account of Richard's last months which is in startling contrast to the authenticity of the preceding narrative.[64]

The curious statement in the Chronicle that Norfolk, Ratclyffe, Brackenbury, and John Kendall fled the field of battle when Richard was killed[65] has often been cited as evidence in support of the theory of a second writer. Alison Hanham offers another, quite plausible explanation for this discrepancy. She discovered, in comparing a seventeenth-century transcription of the Chronicle now in the Bodleian Library with the printed version, the omission of several important words following the names of Norfolk and the others. These words, which tell of the death in battle of these loyal supporters of the king, immediately precede the chronicler's report of the defection of some of the northerners in whom Richard had placed such trust. Thus, the omission of a few words by a careless printer has, Hanham believes, unfairly stigmatized the writer of this Continuation as unreliable or deliberately untruthful.[66]

It seems strange, when one remembers the deformed hunchback of the Tudor tradition, that not one of the afore-mentioned writers felt it necessary to describe Richard's

physical appearance. He was described, however, by Nicho-
las von Poppelau, the last of the trio of foreign contemporaries who wrote with any degree of personal knowledge about
the king.   Poppelau was a Silesian diplomat who visited the
English court in May 1484 and in his travel diary he jotted
down what may be the only surviving eye-witness description
of Richard.   The English king, he wrote, was three fingers
taller than himself, but thinner, leaner, and not so thickset.
His arms and legs were delicate, and he had a great heart.[67]
Because Poppelau was noted for his enormous strength, C.
A. J. Armstrong, who printed this description in the Appendix to Mancini's work, draws the unwarranted conclusion
that Richard was probably quite tall.   This leads Armstrong
to the rather surprising theory that Richard must have been
considerably tall, stooped, and emaciated.[68]

          This small collection of fact, rumor, and conjecture
is the seed from which sprang the Tudor myth.   It may,
perhaps, more properly be called a spindly plant onto which
were grafted the strong and enduring branches of this fas-
cinating legend.   It is not difficult to trace the growth of
this tradition because, unlike many of the historical myths
which arise out of chance incidents or apocryphal stories,
this one may have been, at least in the beginning, a deliberate and purposeful invention.   Why and how this was done
may become apparent through an examination of the Tudor
sources.

          The first words written about Richard III after his
death did not become a part of the legend.   When the news
of the Battle of Bosworth reached the city of York on the following day, the Recorder inscribed an obituary to the late
king in the city Register.

              It was shown by divers persons, especially by
              John Spon, sent unto the field of Redmore, to
              bring tidings from the same to the city, that King
              Richard, late lawfully reigning over us, was,
              through great treason of the Duke of Norfolk, and
              many others that turned against him, with many
              other lords and nobility of the north parts, piteous-
              ly slain and murdered, to the great heaviness of
              this city.[69]

It was, of course, the Duke of Northumberland and not Norfolk who committed the great treason, but whether the substitution of names was deliberate, or the result of misinforma-

tion, cannot be determined. Henry Tudor was to discover,
however, that as long as men lived who remembered the late
king, Richard retained the affection of the Yorkshiremen he
had loved so well.

Richard's bodily deformity, which was viewed by generations of writers as the physical manifestation of a corrupt and evil personality, is one of the earliest and most
enduring aspects of the legend. John Rous, a chaplain at
Guy's Cliffe in Warwickshire, was the inventor of the story
of Richard's strange birth and repulsive appearance, which
he included in his Historia Regum Angliae, a work written
after Richard's death.[70] Rous, who has not unfairly been
called a time-server,[71] followed the policy of praising ef-
fusively whichever monarch currently reigned. He described
Richard during his lifetime as

> a mighty prince and especial good lord, ... in
> his realm full commendably punishing offenders of
> the laws, especially oppressors of his commons,
> and cherishing those that were virtuous, by the
> which discreet guiding he got great thanks and love
> of all his subjects rich and poor, and great laud
> of the people of all other lands about him.[72]

After Henry's victory at Bosworth, Rous obviously felt that
he could best serve his new master by destroying the reputation of his predecessor. He excised the passage praising
Richard from his copy of the Rous Rolls but was unable to
alter one which had passed into other hands.[73] In the Historia Regum Angliae, however, Rous made amends for his
past errors. He accused Richard of murdering Henry VI,
his two nephews, and his wife Anne[74] and described him as
a "monster and tyrant, born under a hostile star and perish-
ing like Antichrist,"[75] who, after remaining two years in
his mother's womb, emerged finally with teeth, hair down
to his shoulders, talons, and a hump.[76] Rous's work is
considered of little historical value except for his contribution of this fantastic story to the Ricardian legend.[77]

Bernard André, the tutor of Henry VII's son Arthur,
and royal historiographer, added little of either fact or
rumor to the legend. In his Life of Henry VII, written at
the king's request between 1500 and 1503, André, however,
indicated the direction which future Tudor writers were to
take. The infant monster invented by Rous becomes the
bloodthirsty child, the enfant terrible who takes as much

pleasure in cruelty as other children do in games. Opposed
to Richard, the embodiment of evil, is Henry Tudor, portrayed by André as the almost saintly symbol of virtue. [78]
The concept of a poor but noble leader sent by heaven to
save England from destruction by the Prince of Darkness
was certainly not discouraged by the Tudors.   As a simple,
but effective device with which to make a moral point or
stress dramatic contrast, it was employed by chroniclers,
poets, and playwrights long after the Tudor period.

  Polydore Vergil, an Italian cleric who came to England in 1502, was the first writer to attempt a comprehen-
sive history which did not follow the form of the chronicles
or annals.   The result was the Anglica Historia, begun at
Henry's request about 1507 and published in 1534.   This
first edition contained 26 books and covered English history
up to 1509. [79]   For the period preceding the reign of Edward
IV, Vergil used published English and French sources, add-
ing no new information and perpetuating many errors of
chronology and fact. [80]   It was Vergil's use, or misuse of
sources of information on the Yorkist period, however, which
has subjected him to some very harsh criticism.   He has
been accused of deficiency in judgment, partiality, and gross
falsehood, [81] and many writers have charged that he burned
manuscripts and other histories, with Henry VII's authority,
in order to hide the faults in his work. [82]   It is, perhaps,
unfair to dismiss Vergil, as one recent writer did, as a
"paid liar," [83] but it must be borne in mind that he was
writing for a patron who had displaced Richard III on the
throne.

  Vergil was the first of the English historians to accuse Richard, in concert with Clarence and Hastings, of
having murdered Prince Edward after the Battle of Tewkesbury. [84]   The young prince, declares Vergil, who probably
used a French source for the incident, [85] was brought before
the king after the battle.   Edward demanded to know how the
prince was so bold as to enter his realm and make war.
The prince replied that he had come to recover his inheritance, at which bold answer the king thrust him away and
the three noblemen "crewelly murderyd" the brave youth. [86]
The story was readily adopted by other writers and thus became a part of the legend.   It is interesting to note that
Robert Fabyan, whose Chronicles were first published in
1516, recounted the same incident with one rather significant
difference.   The young prince, according to Fabyan, "was
by the kynges servauntes incontynently slayne. "[87]

These two contemporary writers are in complete accord, however, about the death of Henry VI. Since neither of them had first-hand knowledge of the event they apparently accepted the rumor which accorded best with the characterization of Richard III which was developing during this period. Fabyan reports that diverse tales were told of the death of Henry "but the moost comon fame wente, that he was stykked with a dagger, by the handes of the duke of Gloucester."[88] Vergil, who places Henry's death after the defeat of the Bastard of Fauconberg,* declares that the "countynuall report is, that Richerd duke of Gloucester killyd him with a swoord, whereby his brother might be delyvered from all fears of hostyleytie."[89]

In his narrative Fabyan gives few details of the events following the death of Edward IV and a curious flatness of style tends to make each appear equally important. Indeed, Fabyan places little more emphasis on the story of the murder of the princes than on any other incident he recounts. He declares that when Richard seized the throne he lost the love and admiration of the nobles who then "murmered and grudgeyd agayne him."[90] By the second year of the reign, the nobles' discontent had greatly increased, "and the more for asmoche as the common fame went that kynge Richarde hadde within the Tower put unto secret deth the ii sonnes of his broder Edward the iiii."[91] It was the suspected murder of the princes, according to Fabyan, which caused Buckingham to revolt against the king.[92]

Vergil gives a more detailed account of the events which led up to Richard's seizure of the crown and the death of the princes. Richard, "who thought of nothing but tyrannie and crueltie,"[93] had determined at the time of his brother's death to seize the crown.[94] In order to achieve his ambition it was necessary to gain custody of the two young princes. As soon as he learned from Hastings of his brother's death and his appointment as Protector, he hurried south accompanied by "no smaule force of armyd men."[95] Richard met the young king and his "smaule trayne" at

---

*The Bastard of Fauconberg, a relative of the Earl of Warwich, led an assault upon London early in May 1471. His forces were driven back and Fauconberg fled to Sandwich. After Henry's death, on May 21, Richard pursued the rebels who submitted to the king and received his pardon. Fauconberg was executed, for a new act of treason, several months later. --P. M. Kendall, Richard III, pp. 120-121, 125.

Stony Stratford, arrested Rivers and Grey, and proceeded to
London. [96] Once there, he convinced the council that the
Duke of York must be removed from sanctuary to attend his
brother's coronation "and so was thinnocent chyld pullyd owt
of his mothers armes."[97]

By then Richard decided that Hastings, who had begun to suspect the Protector's motives, must be done away
with. At the council meeting following York's removal from
sanctuary, Richard accused the queen and Hastings of using
witchcraft to destroy his health and cause parts of his body
to fall away. He displayed his arm to prove his contention,
and Hastings was executed without trial. [98]

Having thus disposed of the major obstacles in his
path, Richard then persuaded Ralph Shaa to preach a sermon
at Paul's Cross in which he declared Richard to be the only
lawfully begotten son of the late Duke of York. [99] Vergil
denies what he calls the "common report" that Shaa had declared the children of Edward IV to be illegitimate and
claims that Richard slandered only his own mother. [100]
Buckingham, acting under Richard's orders, then addressed
the magistrates and nobles, demanding that the crown be
given to the rightful heir. [101]

After his coronation, Richard went to Gloucester and
it was there, according to Vergil, that he "determynyd by
death to dispatche his nephewys, because so long as they
lyved he could never be out of hazard."[102] Brackenbury
was ordered, but refused to kill the princes, and so the
king sent Tyrell to London to carry out the wicked scheme.
Tyrell murdered the two boys, but Vergil does not know by
what means this was accomplished. [103]

There can be little doubt that the man most responsible for the wide acceptance of the Tudor myth was Sir
Thomas More. His History of Richard the Third, written
about 1513, marks the appearance of the first real history of
literary merit written in English[104] as well as the true beginning of the Tudor tradition. [105] The work first appeared
in print in 1543, in Grafton's Continuation of Hardyng's
Chronicle. [106] It was reprinted in 1548 as part of Hall's
Chronicle[107] and an authentic version was published by
More's nephew, William Rastell, in 1557. [108] Few histories
have raised a greater storm of controversy. Almost every-
thing about The History of Richard the Third has been called
into question, including the identity of the author, his motive

for writing the work, and the sources upon which it was
based.   Most, though by no means all historians, however,
agree that More wrote the <u>History</u> and based it largely on
information supplied him by Richard's old enemy, Bishop
Morton.[109]   More's reputation as a man of great honor and
integrity has been cited as an argument to "prove" both the
general reliability of the <u>History</u> and, contrarily, the impossibility of such a piece of false and malicious propaganda's
having been written by such a man.   Paul Murray Kendall,
in his discussion of this apparent contradiction, declares:

> The gross inaccuracies of this work, its apparently
> willful distortions of fact and its urgent bias, are
> not nearly so surprising as the positive virulence
> which informs it.   Richard is entirely removed
> from the sphere of human life; he is evil incarnate,
> sheer monster, and as such he is reviled.[110]

The fact that Morton supplied most of the information for the
<u>History</u>, Kendall declares, only partially explains More's
caricature of Richard.   Kendall conjectures that More's in-
tense dislike of the dark and scheming side of Henry VII's
character may have led him to portray Richard, the last
monarch of an extinct dynasty, as an example and a warning
to other princes.[111]

More's description of Richard, which incorporated
Rous's story of his long gestation and strange appearance at
birth, became the model for generations of writers.   He
was, says More,

> little of stature, ill-fetured of limmes, croke-
> backed, his left shoulder much higher then his
> right, hard-favoured of visage and suche as is in
> states called warlye and in other menne otherwise.
> He was malicious, wrathful, envious, and from
> afore his birth, ever frowarde.   ... Hee was
> close and secrete, a deepe dissimuler, lowlye of
> counteynaunce, arrogant of heart.[112]

Richard's shrivelled and withered arm, which he exposed at
the famous council meeting of June 13,[113] was another invention which More added to what had already become a
totally unbelievable monster.

More is the first writer to accuse Richard of murdering Henry VI on his own authority, and without Edward's

consent.[114] He is the first also to hint at Richard's complicity in Clarence's death, although admitting that the accusation did not rest on a substantial basis of fact.[115] The
charge was quickly incorporated into the legend and, by the
end of the sixteenth century, Richard was generally pictured
as not only desiring Clarence's death, as More claimed,[116]
but also as being his actual murderer.[117]

The addition of Jane Shore to the list of Richard's
victims is another of More's innovations. The dramatic story
he tells of this kindhearted woman, despoiled of her possessions and forced to do public penance by the cruel Protector,[118] was eagerly seized upon, especially by writers of
fiction, during the sixteenth century.

More's version of Dr. Shaa's sermon both supports
and contradicts Vergil's account. Both writers agree that
Richard slandered his mother with the contention that he was
his father's only lawfully begotton son[119] but, whereas Vergil
specifically denies that Shaa declared the children of Edward
IV to be illegitimate, More gives in detail the story of Edward's pre-contract. However, by substituting the name of
Elizabeth Lucy,[120] one of Edward's many mistresses and the
mother of two of his children,[121] for the name of Eleanor
Butler, the daughter of the Earl of Shrewesbury and the
woman named in Titulus Regius,[122] More succeeded in ob-
scuring the facts and casting an air of rather ridiculous im-
probability over the incident.

The high point of More's History is his detailed and
largely implausible story of the murder of the princes in
the Tower. Before he begins his tale, More makes two
rather interesting admissions. He declares that he has
heard many different stories about the fate of the princes
but has chosen this particular version as the one he believed
to be true.[123] This follows the rather surprising statement
that many people in that time remained in doubt about whether or not the princes had been destroyed during Richard's
reign.[124] Brushing aside these doubts, however, More relates substantially the same story as the one told by Vergil,
with one very important exception. Vergil named the mur-
derers; More tells how the murders were committed. John
Dighton and Miles Forest, acting on Tyrell's orders, smoth-
ered the two boys in their bed and then buried the bodies
under a heap of stones at the foot of a stairway. When
Richard learned of this he commended the deed but disap-
proved the burial place as unfit for a king's sons. The

bodies were thereupon removed by a priest and interred in some secret, and presumably more fitting, place.[125] The many errors and inconsistencies in the story,[126] which More claims to have based on a confession made by Tyrell before his death in 1502,[127] did not prevent its acceptance as fact for centuries after it was written.

The History of Richard the Third ends abruptly in the middle of a conversation between Bishop Morton and the Duke of Buckingham which led ultimately to the duke's unsuccessful rebellion and death. The narrative is taken up by Grafton in his Continuation to Hardyng's Chronicle, relying on Vergil as his chief source. Grafton, in describing the circumstances of Anne's death, mentions almost as an aside the possibility that she may have been poisoned,[128] but adds little else of importance to the legend.

The chronicle written by Edward Hall, entitled The Union of the Two Noble and Illustre Famelies of Lancastre and Yorke, was of the greatest importance in the further development of the legend, for it was this work, either directly or through Holinshed's Chronicles, that influenced Shakespeare's view of history. Hall's Chronicles, first published in 1548, was compiled from many French and English sources, including the works of More and Vergil, and was "intended as a glorification of the House of Tudor."[129] All of the crimes attributed to Richard by earlier Tudor writers are recounted in substantially the same words, but Grafton's statement that Anne may have been poisoned is, in Hall's work, "affirmed to be most likely."[130]

At the Battle of Bosworth, Hall pictures Richard addressing a long harangue to his troops in which he admitted that he had yielded to sinister council and diabolical temptation and committed a detestable act in order to obtain the crown. He has expiated and purged the offense, he told them, and demanded that they forget it, even while deploring and lamenting it.[131] Because they hated Richard, the soldiers were unable or unwilling to forgive his crime and deserted in large numbers.[132]

Opposed to the monstrously evil Richard is Henry Tudor who, Hall declares, was "so formed and decorated with all gyftes and lyniamentes of nature that he seemed more an angelical creature than a terrestriall personage."[133] Henry had the further advantage of fighting in a just cause against "a Capitayne, beynge an homicide and murderer of

hys owne bloude and progenye," who had usurped Henry's
"laweful patrymonye and lyneall inhertyaunce. For he that
calleth hym selfe Kynge, kepeth from me the Crowne and
regymente of this noble realme and countrey contrarye to all
justice and equitie. "[134]

Hall's obituary for Richard differs radically from the
one written into the York City Records. According to Hall:

> When his death was knowen, few lamented, and
> many rejoyced, the proude braggyng white bore
> (which was his badge) was violently rased and
> plucked downe from every signe and place where
> it myght be espied, so yll was his lyfe that men
> wished the memorie of hym to be buried with his
> carren corps. [135]

The Chronicles of England, Scotland, and Ireland by
Raphael Holinshed, published in 1578, adds little to Hall's
Chronicles save for a rather pontifical judgment on the sins
of the House of York. "The House of Yorke shewed it selfe
more bloudie in seeking to obteine the kingdome, than that
of Lancaster in usurping it," and the punishment of God was
the destruction of the male line of York. [136]

Francis Bacon, who served in government posts under
the last Tudor and the first Stuart monarchs, wrote in 1622
a History of the Reign of King Henry VII which deviated not
at all from established tradition. After Bosworth, he explains:

> Though the king of his nobleness gave charge unto
> the friars of Leicester to see an honourable inter-
> ment to be given to it [i.e., Richard's corpse],
> yet the religious people themselves being not free
> from the humours of the Vulgar, neglected it;
> wherein nevertheless they did not then incur any
> man's blame or censure: no man thinking any
> ignominy or contumely unworthy of him that had
> been the executioner of King Henry the Sixth, that
> innocent prince, with his own hands; the contriver
> of the death of the Duke of Clarence, his brother;
> the murderer of his two nephews, one of them his
> lawful king in the present, and the other in the fu-
> ture, failing of him; and vehemently suspected to
> have been the impoisoner of his wife, thereby to
> make vacant his bed, for a marriage within the de-
> grees forbidden. [137]

Bacon is not so naive or unscholarly as to accept entirely the black and white picture presented in the chronicles of the fifteenth century. Richard, he admits, was a good warrior and a good lawmaker, whose virtues, which Bacon believes were probably feigned, were outweighed by his vices.[138] If Richard was not pure evil, neither was Henry pure good. His title to the crown was doubtful, Bacon admits,[139] and his treatment of his wife shabby. Henry resented his wife's popularity and hated the House of York, and those feelings can only have been intensified by the rebellion in the north in 1486. Henry knew, declares Bacon, that the men in those parts "were not only affectionate to the house of York, but particularly had been devoted to King Richard the Third."[140] The flaws noticed in Henry Tudor and the few small virtues accorded Richard by Francis Bacon cannot be viewed as an attack on the Tudor myth, but they do represent a slightly more critical evaluation of the period than can be found in any sixteenth-century work.

In his Introduction to A Continuation of the Collection of the History of England published in 1636, John Trussell assures the reader that he has "left no Chronicle of this land, that purse, or prayer could purchase or procure, unperused"[141] and that he has forborne to "obtrude upon thee anything of my own invention."[142] This little known but rather delightful work was designed to bridge the gap between Samuel Daniel's History, which ends with the reign of Edward III, and Bacon's History of the Reign of King Henry the Seventh,[143] but it follows more closely the style of the sixteenth-century chronicles.

Trussell does not name his sources, but the influence of Vergil, More, or Hall can be seen on every page. There are, however, some original and interesting additions which, unless they come from one or more works no longer extant, belie the author's claim that he invented nothing new. Richard's opposition to the Treaty of Péquigny,[144] for example, which even his enemies approved, is seen in a sinister light by Trussell. What led Richard to oppose the treaty was not outraged national pride, but fear that his great designs could not be accomplished unless the war were pursued.[145] The logic of this statement will, no doubt, escape all but the most clairvoyant readers.

Trussell assigns Richard a more active role in Clarence's death than even Shakespeare's imagination could invent. As part of the plot to destroy Clarence and seize

the throne, he has Richard, rather than Edward, arrest and
execute Clarence's servants on the charge of sorcery.   When
Clarence complained to Edward, he was thrown into the Tower "where his loving brother Richard (not as it was feared
without the Kings privitie)" drowned him in a butt of malmsey
wine.   The unfortunate victim was then laid on his bed and
people were given to understand that he had died of discontent. [146]

Richard, at Edward's deathbed, is pictured as declaring his intention to forgive his enemies and abide by his
brother's wishes. [147]   This dissimulation was intended, of
course, to lull the suspicions of those loyal to the new king.
From there on the story follows fairly closely the traditional
versions.   Trussel has, however, inserted one peculiarly interesting incident which supposedly took place on the road
from Stony Stratford to London.   Five of Richard's servants,
"manacled and pinioned like Traitours," were displayed in
various places along the road, claiming to be men of high
birth who had been seduced into treason by Earl Rivers and
Lord Grey.   Now repentent, these supposed traitors disavowed
the two noblemen and demanded their execution.   The actors,
using different disguises, repeated this performance all along
the route followed by the young king and his uncle Gloucester. [148]

Trussell's History contains numerous errors in names,
dates, and fact which indicate that he incorporated published
works of fiction as well as chronicles and histories into his
text. *   This is a work, however, of great charm and wit and
makes enjoyable reading as long as it is not taken seriously
as history.

The chapters dealing with the Wars of the Roses in
The History of England by the great Scottish philosopher
David Hume do not differ significantly in tone or content
from any of the chronicles or histories which preceded it.
Hume, who wrote his work in the middle of the eighteenth
century, accepted almost without question the Tudor version

---

*For example, Trussell places Richard in London when Ed-
ward died (p. 25).   He also declares that Richard married
Anne after he took the throne (p. 227).   This repeats a
similar error in Heywood's Edward IV, Part II.   (See be-
low, p. 83.)   Trussell also copies Hall's dating of the
Battle of Bosworth as August 22, 1486.   Compare Trussell's
Continuation, p. 251 with Hall's Chronicles, p. 419.

of the events, despite the fact that contradictory documents
and records had, by that time, come to light. Richard appears as a "bloody and treacherous tyrant"[149] whose body
was "in every particular no less deformed then his mind,"[150]
and whose title to the throne was "never acknowledged by any
national assembly."[151] He was guilty of every murder
charged against him by the Tudor writers except, perhaps,
that of Henry VI. Although there is no proof of his guilt,
Hume explains, Richard is generally blamed for this murder
because "the universal odium which that prince has incurred
inclined perhaps, the nation to aggravate his crimes without
any sufficient authority."[152]

Three-quarters of a century before Hume wrote his
History, a chest containing the bones of two children was
discovered beneath a staircase outside the White Tower.
The remains were assumed to be those of the two princes
and were subsequently interred in Westminster Abbey.   This
discovery appears to contradict More's assertion that the
bodies of the princes were removed from their hiding place
under the stairs and reinterred elsewhere.   Hume reconciles
this apparent contradiction by explaining that the priest whom
Richard ordered to rebury the bodies in a more suitable
place may have died before he was able to accomplish his
task.[153] Thus Hume ties up all the loose ends, leaves the
Tudor myth undisturbed, and dismisses a period of English
history which he found distasteful in the extreme.[154]

The savage and frequent attacks on the reputation of
Richard III in the three centuries following his death did not
pass completely unchallenged.   The first published defense,
"The Prayse of King Richard the Third," appeared in 1616
as one of the Essayes of Certaine Paradoxes of William
Cornwallis.   At least one modern authority has argued that
this work was actually written shortly after Bosworth in answer to Morton's attack on Richard and was merely appro-
priated by Cornwallis.[155] He bases his contention on the
fact that four earlier manuscript copies of this work appear
to have been written by one of Richard's contemporaries,
not as a generalized attack on Tudor historians, but as a
specific answer to a single writer.[156] Most historians,
however, accept Cornwallis as the author of the essay.

Cornwallis rejects much of the Tudor tradition and
attempts to justify those allegations which he concedes might
possibly be true.   He accepts as fact Richard's misshapen
form which he declares was a blessing in that nature com-

pensated for it by forming his mind more perfectly. [157]
Richard had no part in the deaths of Clarence or Prince Edward, and there is no proof of his having murdered Henry
VI.   If he was responsible for Henry's murder, however, it
only proves his love for his brother. [158]   In the same vein,
Cornwallis declares that if Richard killed the princes, "by
doing the deed he freed the people from dissension, and how
better could he prove his love than by risking his soul for
their quiet?"[159]

Richard is praised as discreet, brave, merciful, wise,
and a maker of good laws.   All of his virtues, Cornwallis
complains, have been ignored by historians or dismissed as
"enamellers of vices."[160]   The author closes his spirited
defense of Richard with the words: "Yet for all this know,
I hold this but a Paradox."[161]   These words and the fact
that this essay is followed by one in praise of the "French
Pockes," have convinced some historians that Cornwallis did
not intend his defense of Richard to be taken seriously.   A.
R. Myers has termed it "an exercise in rhetoric to defend
the indefensible,"[162] but this view is by no means universal.

There is no question that The History of the Life and
Reigne of Richard III by Sir George Buck was intended as a
serious defense.   Buck, whose ancestor had been executed
after Bosworth for fighting for Richard, was Master of Rev-
els during the reign of James I.   He wrote the work in 1619,
but died three years later without having published it.   The
manuscript came eventually into the hands of his great-neph-
ew, another George Buck, who altered and cut the work in
an attempt to pass it off as his own. [163]   The History was
published in 1646 with its original spirit and much of its
content intact. [164]

Buck's work has been called "blundering and uncritical and as prejudiced in its direction as the tradition it attacks,"[165] and it is quite true that it contains many errors
in fact and judgment.   Despite its flaws, however, the importance of this work cannot be minimized.   Buck attacked
not just the Tudor legend itself, but the men who had created it.   He was the first writer to point up and attack the
prejudiced sources on which the Tudor tradition is based.
Referring to More's History he declares, "Doctor Morton
... made the Booke, and Master More ... set it forth,
amplifying and glossing it."[166]   Buck severely criticizes the
historians and chroniclers who had accepted the authority of
a man whose reputation for piety and learning was, in his
opinion, greatly exaggerated.[167]

Buck was the first writer to make use of the Croyland Chronicle[168] and the Titulus Regius in order to prove that Edward's pre-contract was with Eleanor Talbot, rather than Elizabeth Lucy. [169]   He pronounces Richard innocent of all crimes charged against him by the Tudor writers.   Indeed, Buck declares the greatest of the alleged crimes to have been no crime at all.   The sons of Edward IV were not murdered by anyone.   Edward, the elder of the boys, was a sickly youth and probably died a natural death. [170]   Richard, the younger, was secretly conveyed into a foreign country only to reappear many years later as Perkin Warbeck. [171] Buck uses some persuasive arguments to support his case and repeats Cornwallis's charge that Richard's many virtues were condemned as vices by his Tudor enemies.   "Malice and ignorance have been the Kings greatest accusers," he declares. [172]

Unfortunately, much of the force of Buck's argument is weakened by errors of fact, dates, and chronology, * and by the use of documents whose very existence has been called into question. †   For these, and other less important reasons, this work has been justifiably criticized, but it does appear to be going rather too far to claim, as A. R. Myers has done, that "except for his criticism of More, Buck's defense of Richard III does not amount to much."[173]

Whether Buck's defense amounted to much or not, more than a century after the author's death his work made one rather important convert.   In 1768 Horace Walpole published Historic Doubts on the Life and Reign of King Richard the Third, and if he added little knowledge to the subject he can be credited with having begun a debate which continues unabated to the present day.   There are great weaknesses in Walpole's arguments since he lacked many of the documents which have come to light since his time.   He

---

*For example, in his Life and Reigne of Richard III, Buck places Buckingham's rebellion in 1484 (p. 31), states that Richard was at the Battle of Mortimer's Cross (p. 9), and declares that the young Duke of York was removed from sanctuary at the end of May 1483 (p. 11).

†For example, the supposed letter from Elizabeth of York to the Duke of Norfolk, declaring her love for Richard (p. 128). There has been much controversy over whether Buck actually saw this letter and if he did, whether or not it was a forgery.

did, however, make use of such sources as were available, including the Croyland Chronicle[174] and a fifteenth-century Wardrobe account which he mistakenly believed to be Richard's Coronation Roll. [175]

Walpole attacks the Tudor tradition point by point, comparing the versions of each of Richard's alleged crimes given by contemporary authorities with those of later Tudor writers. Like Buck, he acquits him of every charge, arguing not only lack of evidence to support Richard's guilt, but also contending that the commission of such crimes would have been inconsistent with Richard's normal behavior pattern and against his interest. [176] Walpole follows Buck in attacking the weaknesses in More's version of the death of the princes and he, too, tends to the belief that the boys were not murdered. [177] He declares that not only was Perkin Warbeck the true Duke of York, but also that Henry VII's behavior in the affair tends to show that he believed the youth was not an imposter. [178]

Walpole's vindication of Richard met with an immediate storm of criticism and abuse from the author's contemporaries who found his arguments unconvincing and his subject unworthy of defense. [179] In the absence of sufficient documentary proof, both Walpole and Buck fell back on logic and reason to discredit the Tudor historians. Indeed, this was probably the greatest contribution these two writers made to succeeding generations of historians. Diligent research by scholars has greatly increased the knowledge and understanding of this confused and violent period, but it was Buck and Walpole who first demonstrated the basic unreliability of the Tudor legend. Certainly, they did not prove Richard III innocent of the crimes charged against him, but they did show that the Tudor historians had not proved him guilty.

Five

THE LATER HISTORIANS

> The evil that men do lives after them,
> The good is oft interred with their bones.
> --Julius Caesar III, ii.

The arguments of Buck and Walpole made no impression on John Lingard, the Catholic clergyman and historian who published his many-volumed History of England in the early nineteenth century. Lingard accepted without question the one-dimensional Tudor view of Richard as a monster of evil who had no redeeming qualities. He saw no reason to dispute Hall's version of the death of Edward of Lancaster, despite the fact that it is at odds with contemporary accounts. [1] The true story of the death of Henry VI, Lingard declares, could only be told by Tudor writers who no longer had to fear Yorkist vengeance. By that time it was safe, not only to proclaim the murder, but to attribute it to the "advice, if not the dagger" of the Duke of Gloucester. [2]

Lingard does not mention Richard in connection with Clarence's death, [3] but he has no doubt that this prince, who was "little better than a monster in human shape," [4] slandered his mother, [5] murdered his nephews in the manner described by More, [6] and poisoned his wife so that he could marry his niece. [7] It is rather interesting that the only piece of Buck's "evidence" which Lingard is willing to accept is the uncorroborated story of Elizabeth's letter to Norfolk. [8] The letter, he declares, indicates, if it does not prove, that Richard poisoned his wife in order to marry Elizabeth. [9]

Lingard quite obviously believed in the sanctity of the Tudor tradition despite the proven bias of its source. He peremptorily dismisses the challenges of Buck and Walpole by declaring that writers who have attempted to prove Richard innocent of the charges laid against him are shown to be

wrong when confronted with the evidence.[10]   Since Lingard's
evidence consists of the works of More, Rous, Hall, and
other Tudor writers, he ends up right where he started and
adds nothing to what was already known.

The History of England During the Middle Ages by
Sharon Turner presents a marked contrast to Lingard's History.   Turner made use of many sources unknown to, or ignored by previous historians and he maintains throughout his
work a rare critical detachment.   Turner emphasizes the
fact that no contemporary writer accused Richard of the murder of Prince Edward,[11] and he considers it quite unlikely
that Richard was responsible for the death of Henry VI.[12]
Richard was then only eighteen years old and, Turner believes, he was not likely to have been an assassin at that age.
Furthermore, as the king's brother and a recently proved
general, he was so much in the public eye, he could hardly
have gone unnoticed to the Tower.   Turner's final argument
against Richard's having committed this crime is that Rivers
was then Constable of the Tower and would almost certainly
have publicly censured Richard for such an act.[13]   Indeed,
Turner believes that Henry died a natural death, having been
weakened by a previous assassination attempt and by the
hopelessness of his position.[14]

It was more likely, Turner believes, that the Duke of
Clarence, for whose death Richard has frequently been held
directly or indirectly responsible, may have been a victim
of the "vindictive policy" of the Woodvilles.[15]   Indeed, he
observes that it was the apparent object of the Tudor chroniclers to make Richard's memory an "execration among man-
kind" and to achieve this end his motives and actions were
distorted, his faults exaggerated, and his virtues denied.[16]
Turner's criticism extends, in a milder form, to Richard's
defenders as well.   He finds Buck's work too feeble and
"random" and Walpole's too partisan and insufficiently researched.[17]

Turner recognizes that Richard was merely the "creature and mirror" of a violent age,[18] who reacted to a very
real danger in much the same way that any of his peers
would have done.[19]   The fact that Richard had the support
of most of the great men of the kingdom for his actions does
not, declares Turner, excuse those actions.[20]   There was
no legal or moral justification for Richard's usurpation even
though it was an act which "few censured; most applauded,"
and one in which "all acquiesced."[21]   Turner believes that

the bones found in the Tower tend to support More's version
of the death of the princes, despite the inconsistencies in the
story. [22]   He does not doubt that Richard deeply regretted
killing his nephews and attempted to expiate the crime by
becoming a good and just ruler. [23]

Whereas the Tudor writers saw in Richard's death at
Bosworth Field at the hands of Henry Tudor the triumph of
good over evil, Turner refuses to accept such a simplistic
explanation.   Richard was betrayed, he declares, by the
very men who had benefitted most from his generosity and
who therefore owed him the greatest loyalty.   According to
the Tudor writers, the actions of these nobles must be attributed to revulsion against Richard's criminal behavior.
Turner is probably more accurate in ascribing their treason
to ambition and self-interest.

> Thus fell Richard, the victim of treachery un-
> paralleled; for there seems to have been no na-
> tional movement in favor of Richmond.   It was a
> perfidious combination of five noblemen which de-
> stroyed Richard. . . .   The nation had no share in
> the conflict, notwithstanding all that is said of the
> king's unpopularity. . . .   Whatever had been his
> conduct towards his nephew, he had done nothing
> to them to deserve that they should have destroyed
> him.   But it was the religious ordinance of the
> moral governor of human life, that a crown which
> had been usurped by crime and treachery should
> be torn from the usurper by criminality and per-
> fidy. [24]

Whether or not one agrees with all of his conclusions,
it would not be an exaggeration to credit Turner's careful
scholarship and critical detachment with having set a higher
standard of historical writing than had hitherto been known.

Turner's moderate tone was adopted by John Heneage
Jesse, an amateur and less scholarly historian, who published in 1862 his Memoirs of the Court of England: King
Richard the Third and Some of His Contemporaries.   Jesse
praises Richard's devotion and loyalty to his brother Edward[25] and assails as false and malicious the accounts in
which the Tudor writers implicated Richard in the murders
of Prince Edward, [26] Henry VI, [27] and Clarence. [28]   Jesse,
like Turner, sees Richard as the product of violent and
treacherous times[29] but, unlike Turner, he finds in this

some justification for the usurpation. Jesse argues that
since the throne was virtually elective, Richard was able to
seize it with the consent of the great men of the kingdom
who were anxious to avert a civil war they feared inevitable
under a king who was a minor. [30] There is furthermore, he
declares, no evidence that the usurpation met with any dis-
approval or resistance from the clergy, nobility, or commons. [31]

Despite Jesse's praise for Richard's many accomplishments and his rejection of much of the Tudor tradition
he, like Turner, accepts More's story of the death of the
little princes as true. [32] Quite obviously Jesse, in common
with many other nineteenth-century historians, was very
much influenced by Turner's work. Both Jesse and Turner
believed Richard guilty of the terrible crime of murdering
his innocent nephews, yet neither writer accepted, as did
Lingard, the totally depraved monster of legend.

In 1844 Caroline Halsted launched an all-out attack
on the Tudor tradition in her "Personal Memoir" entitled
Richard III. as Duke of Gloucester and King of England.
Her work is extensively researched but flawed by an almost
total lack of objectivity. She, like Turner, sees Richard as
a product of evil times, but in her explanation his seizure
of the crown is not excused by this fact alone. Halsted believes that the York children were imbued from the cradle
with their mother's inordinate pride[33] and were taught "to
consider a crown as the ultimatum of human happiness, and
its attainment the sole object and chief business of life."[34]
Richard, however, despite his mother's evil influence, became "mild, affable, courteous, pious, charitable, high-
spirited," and was "possessed of shining abilities, and stout
of heart."[35]

Halsted rejects, as unsupported by contemporary evidence, Richard's guilt in connection with all the crimes attributed to him by earlier writers and declares that he would
never have usurped the throne had he not heeded the advice
of evil councillors and allowed himself to be used by treacherous and time-serving allies. [36] Indeed, she avers that
Richard might be considered a usurper in a moral, but not
in a legal and constitutional sense, since he gained the
throne without violence and kept it without open rebellion.
If there is any blame attached to the act, Halsted declares,
it belongs to the peers who deposed Edward V and gave the
throne to Richard. [37]

The discovery of the bones in the Tower which convinced Turner and Jesse of the probable truth of More's version of the death of the princes, had quite the opposite effect on Halsted. More, she points out, had told how the boys' bodies were removed from the Tower and buried in a more suitable grave, and therefore the bones in the Tower were of no significance. She therefore dismisses his account as improbable and inconsistent as were all of the Tudor versions of the episode. She agrees with Buck that the boys were probably sent out of the country for safekeeping and the story of their murder invented by Richard's enemies. [38]

Halsted's impassioned defense of Richard III was followed some forty years later by an almost equally sympathetic, but more moderate and balanced work by Alfred O. Legge, entitled The Unpopular King: The Life and Times of Richard III. While Legge's Richard is not the paragon of virtue portrayed by Halsted, he emerges as an able man of overriding ambition who "loved power for its own sake."[39] It was his desire to remain in a position of power which led Richard to commit the only two acts which Legge considers crimes: the execution of Hastings[40] and the seizure of the crown.[41] Although Legge agrees with Halsted in placing much of the blame for the usurpation on the parliament which deposed Edward V,[42] he believes that Richard must bear the greater share. "The dazzling lustre of a crown had corrupted his moral sense."[43] Legge, however, mitigates his criticism by stressing that Richard took the crown with the consent and approval of the nation.[44] Moreover, he is convinced that, had the Woodvilles remained in power, Richard's life would have been in jeopardy.[45]

Despite his censure of some of Richard's actions, Legge rejects those accusations of the Tudor writers which are unsupported by fact. In their attempt to blacken Richard's name, Legge declares, these writers blamed him for every illegal and violent act committed in his lifetime.[46] More's account of the death of the princes he dismisses as "more than improbable." This often told story, Legge insists, is "full of impossibilities."[47] The fate of the princes, he concludes, is an insoluble mystery,[48] but he offers as the likeliest solution the theory that unscrupulous men like Lovell, Catesby, and Ratcliffe, with the connivance of Brackenbury, murdered the princes while Richard was on progress. It is possible, he believes, that Ratcliffe committed the murders under orders from Buckingham,[49] whose purpose was to ruin Richard by casting the blame on

him.[50]   The bones in the Tower were not the remains
of the princes, Legge declares, but were more probably
those of two of the many menials or prisoners who had died
there.[51]

Legge admires Richard as a man of wisdom and
courage whose goal was to heal the wounds of years of
civil war.   Because he failed to achieve his purpose he
became "an object of hatred and unparalleled vituperation,
for the tide of applause ever runs parallel with that of prosperity."[52]

James Gairdner, whose Richard the Third was until quite recently considered the definitive work on the
subject, rejects the moderation of Turner and the bias
of Halsted in favor of the familiar Tudor characterization
of the evil prince.   Gairdner confesses that in his youth
he entertained some doubts about the validity of the traditional view of Richard.   But, he declares, he long
since learned that a skeptical spirit is fatal in the study
of history,[53] and his investigation of the subject convinced
him that the portrait of Richard made familiar by More and
Shakespeare is the true one.   In apology for his youthful error he declares:

> I feel quite ashamed, at this day, to think how I
> mused over this subject long ago, wasting a great
> deal of time, ink and paper, in fruitless efforts to
> satisfy even my own mind that traditional black
> was real historical white, or at worst a kind of
> grey.[54]

Gairdner concedes that the traditional view of Richard, drawn
from scanty contemporary evidence and prejudiced sources,
may be disputed on some minor points.   This does not, however, weaken his conviction that Shakespeare's portrayal is
essentially true and that "Richard was indeed cruel and unnatural beyond the ordinary measure even of those violent
and ferocious times."[55]

The discovery and publication, during the eighteenth
and nineteenth centuries, of many important contemporary
sources, led some historians to reexamine and reevaluate the
previously accepted history of this period.   Gairdner, unwilling or unable to question the cherished tradition, attempted
to use these new sources to reinforce the Tudor myth.   "It

is rather a painful spectacle," observed Paul Murray Kendall of Gairdner, to see "a great historian beginning with a closed tradition instead of with an open mind."[56]

Gairdner admits that there is no evidence that Richard murdered Prince Edward of Lancaster, but he insists that the story cannot safely be declared apocryphal.[57] Guilt for the death of Henry VI, Gairdner believes, must be shared by Richard, Edward, and the council.[58]

Beset by the difficulties he encountered in attempting to reconcile the accounts of the Tudor writers with the more reliable sources which contradict them, Gairdner falls into one trap after another. He declares that Richard's protectorship was "clearly a reign of terror,"[59] and then admits that "in the North, undoubtedly, and perhaps with the common people generally, Richard was at this time highly popular."[60] Gairdner discusses the various versions of Richard's alleged crimes and then apparently chooses the one which best supports his thesis. He admits that Fabyan, a contemporary of Richard's, did not accuse him of slandering his mother, a story later told by More and Vergil. His belief that the tale must be true, however, does not rest on the evidence of these two writers, but on the fact that fifty years later Thomas Cromwell assured the Imperial ambassador that it was so.* Gairdner takes great pains to point out the inconsistencies and errors in More's account of the death of the princes and then declares it to be substantially true.[61]

Gairdner does concede, however, that Richard had a few redeeming qualities. Good laws were passed during his reign, he was loyal in his support of the church, generous even to his enemies,[62] and able as a general.[63] On balance, however, Richard comes out very badly indeed. It is only Gairdner's condemnation of Henry VII

---

*Gairdner, Richard III, p. 81. Mortimer Levine also cites this story as proof of the allegation, but in his version it is the Imperial ambassador who assured Cromwell of its truth. The story should not be labelled apocryphal on the strength of Levine's reversal of the names since his frequent reference to Markham as Marcham tends to show a rather careless handling of his sources. "Richard III--Usurper or Lawful King?," Speculum 34, no. 4 (1959), 397.

for instituting "a tyrannical and often a most cruel government"[64] and his grudging admission of Richard's few virtues which save this portrait from being one etched in stark
black and white.

In 1891 Gairdner's position was vigorously attacked
in the pages of the English Historical Review by Sir Clements
Markham.   Markham's article, "Richard III: A Doubtful Verdict Reviewed," was an abstract of a full-length book, Richard III: His Life and Character, which was eventually published in 1906.[65] Markham's defense of Richard is based,
in large measure, on his contention that it was Morton, "a
treble-dyed traitor and falsifier of History,"[66] who actually
wrote the work attributed to More.   The fact that Morton,
who was at Tewkesbury, did not accuse Richard of the murder of Prince Edward, is cited by Markham as proof that
this crime was an invention of later writers.[67]   The story
apparently originated with Polydore Vergil whom Markham
accuses of misrepresenting the facts to please Henry Tudor
and then destroying those documents which, presumably,
would have disproved his allegations.[68]   Other writers of the
Tudor period are similarly indicted.   "Morton, Polydore
Vergil, Rous, and Fabyan will be found to be dishonest and
untrustworthy narrators, who can be shown to use deception
deliberately, with full knowledge of the truth," declares
Markham.[69]   To explain the errors in the Croyland Chronicle,[70] Markham advances the thesis that the credulous second monk who wrote the last part of the Continuation repeated misinformation which Morton had deliberately given
him.[71]

Markham accepts none of the charges against Richard.
The murders of Prince Edward, Clarence, Anne, and even
Richard's deformity, he declares, were all invented in order
to make more convincing the tale that he murdered the
princes in the Tower.[72]   The real villain was the grasping,
unscrupulous, and corrupt Morton.   He was at the center of
the Hastings-Woodville plot and was thus responsible for
Hastings' death.[73]   It was Morton who supressed the facts,
altered dates,[74] and reversed the chronology of Hastings'
execution and the removal of the young Duke of York from
sanctuary in order to make Richard's charges of treason
appear false and to make him appear a tyrant.[75]   It was
Morton who substituted the name of Elizabeth Lucy for
Eleanor Butler and accused Richard of slandering his
mother.[76]

What was Morton's purpose in inventing such slanderous accusations against the late king? Markham provides a
very simple answer. It must be made to appear that the
princes had been murdered before Henry came to the throne
and Richard would be more readily accepted as the murderer
if he could be blamed for a long list of previous crimes. [77]
Richard had, however, no motive for killing the princes
since parliament had declared them illegitimate, [78] and Markham is convinced that they were living at Sheriff Hutton when
Henry came to the throne. He cites a contemporary docu-
ment referring to garments ordered for the Lord Bastard,
dated March 9, 1485, and expresses the belief that this was
a reference to Edward V. [79] The rumors of the princes'
death mentioned in the Croyland Chronicle are attributed to
Morton, who probably also repeated them to the Chancellor
of France. [80]

With Richard cleared of all the charges against him,
Markham offers another candidate to take his place. When
Henry Tudor usurped the throne and married Elizabeth of
York, Markham explains, it was essential that her brothers
be killed. Elizabeth Woodville probably suspected that her
son-in-law had murdered her sons and this was the reason
for her enforced confinement in the nunnery. [81] Markham believes that the princes were murdered between June 16 and
July 16, 1486, quite probably by Tyrell, who subsequently
received two pardons from the king. It is the double pardon
which convinced Markham that the tale of Tyrell's confession,
as given out by the Tudor writers, was probably true except
for the substitution of Richard's name for Henry's as the
murderer. [82]

Gairdner responded to Markham's article in the English Historical Review in the July 1891 issue of the same
journal. In an article entitled "Did Henry VII Murder the
Princes?" he disputes Markham's contention that Richard's
earlier crimes were invented by Tudor writers in order to
make the murder of the princes more convincing. Quite the
opposite was true, he argues. It was the murder of the
princes that made Richard's earlier crimes more believable. [83] He restates briefly the views set forth in his book
and then firmly, and with great self-assurance, closes the
door to further argument. "I think I have sufficiently
proved," he declares, "that to whitewash Richard III is an
utterly hopeless task."[84]

The Gairdner-Markham debate stirred a great deal of

interest in Richard III, and the influence of both writers
continued well into the twentieth century. Writers who accepted Markham's point of view, the so-called revisionists,
included many amateur historians among whom was Philip
Lindsay, the author of The Tragic King: Richard III. One
of the most ardent disciples of Markham, Lindsay, a self-
proclaimed "Richard-Lover,"[85] wrote his work for the general public rather than for students of history, and he dis-
dains both footnotes and a bibliography,[86] substituting for the
latter a brief annotated list of acknowledgments. The work
is personal, emotional, and unscholarly. Lindsay is bitterly
critical of the Tudor writers and later historians who state
as fact what, in his opinion, are innuendos, lies, rumors,
and speculations. He seems to think it quite acceptable,
however, to intrude his own opinions and speculations,
which are frequently as biased and ill-founded as those he
finds so offensive in others.

Lindsay's work is essentially a restatement of Markham's arguments. Lindsay, however, was present at the
meeting of the Society of Antiquaries on November 30, 1933,
when Professor William Wright and Lawrence Tanner reported the results of their examination of the bones discovered in the Tower during the reign of Charles II.[87] He
found the evidence presented by the two experts totally unconvincing, both scientifically and historically and, after conduct-
ing some research of his own, he attempted a point-by-point
refutation of their findings. He contends that the bones
could just as easily be the remains of girls as of boys,
their exact ages could not be determined, and he believes
they were probably the remains of foundation sacrifices placed
there centuries before the Yorkist period.[88] If the princes
were murdered in Richard's reign, in Lindsay's opinion a
doubtful hypothesis at best, then Buckingham was the most
likely murderer.[89] These, however, are merely some of
this author's random speculations. Lindsay's basic argument follows Markham in almost every particular including
the diatribe against Morton as the real author of More's
History,[90] and his acceptance of the "usurper, murderer,
and liar,"[91] Henry Tudor, as the murderer of the princes.[92]

Another of Richard's defenders influenced by Markham
is Thomas Costain, the prolific writer of popular history and
historical fiction. His The Last Plantagenets is a more
reasoned, and therefore more convincing work than Lindsay's.
Costain does not dispute either More's authorship of the History or his integrity. He does, however, question the sound-

ness of More's historical judgment, declaring that his work reads more like a political broadside than a history. [93] All of More's misinformation came from Bishop Morton, whom Costain denounces as a "conniving servant of a sly master. "[94] Following Markham's arguments, Costain indicts Morton for inventing all of the early crimes in order to make the murder of the princes more convincing. [95] In addition, Costain believes it quite likely the two boys were alive when Henry came to the throne and consequently, Henry had good reason for preventing any investigation concerning their fate. [96] Costain believes that it is possible that Henry may have had the princes killed. [97] He does not, like Lindsay, pronounce it a certainty. The evidence of the bones in the Tower, Costain believes, tends to show that, if they are indeed the remains of the princes, that they died no earlier than 1485. [98]

Costain concedes that the mystery concerning the fate of the princes has not been, and probably never will be solved. His plea is not for a verdict of innocent, but for a fair trial. On the basis of the evidence, he declares, Richard cannot in honesty be accounted guilty. [99]

If Richard must be adjudged not guilty of the murder of the princes, so too must Henry Tudor, declares V. B. Lamb. [100] In The Betrayal of Richard III Lamb reviews the evidence and concludes that there is no proof on which to charge anyone with murder, or even to assume that a murder was committed. [101] Markham's accusation against Henry, he argues, is as untenable as the Tudor charges against Richard. If anyone connected with Henry had killed the princes, it would have been a simple matter to produce the bodies and charge the crime to Richard. Had Henry been able to prove that Warwick was the only surviving male Plantagenet he could have prevented the rebellions which plagued his reign. All of Henry's actions, insists Lamb, tend to prove that he did not know what had become of the princes, and while he may not have believed that Perkin Warbeck was the son of Edward IV, he nevertheless feared that the boys were still alive. [102]

If Henry lacked the opportunity for the murder, Richard lacked the motive. [103] It is quite possible, Lamb believes, that they died natural deaths or were sent into hiding for their own safety. If they were still alive when Henry came to the throne, their continued security lay in anonymity. [104] These are, of course, speculations rather than solutions and they form a significant part of every defense of

Richard III.   It is Lamb's defense of Henry Tudor on the
charge of the murder of the princes that make his work
unique.

The publication, in 1966, of <u>Bosworth Field and the
Wars of the Roses</u> can have done little to enhance the reputation of its author, A. L. Rowse, the noted scholar and
historian of the Tudor period.   Rowse writes with aggressive
self-confidence, stating his opinions as facts and dismissing
with scornful ridicule all writers who hold contrary opinions.
The scholarly and valuable works of Paul Murray Kendall
and Cora Scofield are, along with their authors, sneeringly
brushed aside with the unmistakable implication that they are
of little importance. [105]   Rowse very much prefers to take
his history of this period from More, Shakespeare, and
other traditionalists. [106]

Despite his general acceptance of the Tudor myth,
Rowse concedes a few of the points made by modern scholars.   Richard, he admits, ruled the north efficiently and
well, [107] and had no responsibility for Clarence's death. [108]
Except for these minor points, Richard is the evil and bloody
villain of tradition.   After committing his first crime, the
murder of Henry VI, [109] he declares his intention to marry
Anne Neville.   The young lady, according to Rowse, "had
no wish to marry the unattractive Richard," and rather than
be forced to do so she allowed herself to be concealed as a
kitchen maid by her brother-in-law Clarence. [110]   It is unlikely, however, that Anne was bothered very much after her
marriage by the unwelcome attentions of her husband, for
Richard, Rowse assures us, "was not interested in sex. "[111]

Rowse's evaluation of the sources of the traditional
myth is incredibly naive.   He accepts More's <u>History</u> because the author was "a genius, as well as a saint"[112] and
because everyone knows "what a conscientious and scrupu-
lously truthful man he was. "[113]   He pronounces Hall's portrait of Richard "convincing and just"[114] and declares that
"anyone deriving his view of the whole story from Shakespeare would not be far out. "[115]   Rowse finds Buck's story,
on the other hand, unconvincing and reminds the reader that
"poor Buck ended up out of his mind. "[116]   Indeed, he believes this to be the fate reserved for anyone who defends
Richard.   "There are crackpots about"; Rowse informs us.
"They proliferate in this field as about Shakespeare: people
who do not quality to hold an opinion, much less express
one. "[117]   Rowse, like Gairdner, renders as the final and

irrefutable verdict, that "the traditional picture is in keeping with the best scholarship and the conclusions of common sense."[118]

The views set forth by Rowse echo those of Winston Churchill. Churchill, however, concedes the prejudice of the sources on which the traditional history is based. [119] Nevertheless, he accepts the essential validity of the Tudor myth and rejects as unconvincing the attempts of Richard's defenders to discredit it. Indeed, he fails to see why anyone would waste time in arguing the point. "It will take many ingenious books to raise this issue to the dignity of a historical controversy," he declares. [120]

Any question which has engendered as much debate as has the guilt or innocence of Richard III must be termed a genuine historical controversy, Churchill to the contrary notwithstanding. It is unfortunately quite true that writers on both sides of the issue have occasionally abandoned both dignity and reason in arguing the case. The scholarly and unemotional tone of three of the major works on the fifteenth century provides, therefore, a much needed counterbalance to the often simplistic arguments of the special pleaders.

Lancastrians, Yorkists, and Henry VII by S. B. Chrimes is a brief, but penetrating account of the dynastic struggles of the fifteenth century and the social and economic factors which helped to shape them. The sudden death of Edward IV, Chrimes declares, left a power vacuum which the Woodvilles attempted to fill. As a result, Richard, who had served his brother loyally, found himself in a position of dangerous isolation. [121] Chrimes does not believe that Richard had any responsibility for the deaths of Prince Edward, Henry VI, or Clarence, [122] and he declares that, in view of the enmity of the Woodvilles, he was absolutely right to take control of the young king. [123]

Chrimes argues that the story of the pre-contract was probably true and that Richard himself may have believed it. In any case, he had to have the crown to preserve his life. "It would be a mistake to think of Richard as a mere opportunist," he declares. [124]

Chrimes offers no final solution to the mystery of the fate of the princes. There is insufficient evidence to prove how or when they died, and although he concedes the possibility that they died a natural death, he does not think

it probable.125   Henry, Chrimes declares, would have destroyed the princes had it been necessary, but he finds Richard a more likely candidate.   It was necessary, however,
for Henry to prove that the boys were dead and he attempted
to do this by means of Tyrell's "quite unconvincing confession."126   The evidence of the bones in the Tower is incon-
clusive, Chrimes declares, and unless new facts come to
light there can be no certainty about the fate of the princes.
Until conclusive evidence to the contrary is produced, the
weight of suspicion rests heavily on Richard.127

      If Richard murdered his nephews, it was not a cruel
nature but the pressure of circumstances which dictated the
action.128   Far from being the monster of the Tudor legend,
Chrimes asserts that Richard lacked the ruthlessness which
might have saved his throne.129   Had he treated Margaret
Beaufort and the Stanleys as Henry Tudor did his enemies,130
he might very well have justified his usurpation by a long
and prosperous reign.131

      E. F. Jacob's The Fifteenth Century is a longer and
more detailed work than Chrimes's, although both cover substantially the same period of time.   Jacob examines in depth
the politics and policies of the Lancastrian and Yorkist kings
and concludes that the efficient administration of government,
usually considered a Tudor innovation, was actually a legacy
from the Yorkists.132   Because Richard III is such a controversial figure, Jacob believes, his achievements as a re-
former and innovator in the sphere of justice and order have
been ignored or distorted by many historians.133   Gairdner's
insistence that the murder of the princes makes the other
allegations against Richard more believable gets no support
from Jacob.   "Concentration upon the disappearance of the
two princes should not be the sole determinant of the historian's view of Richard III," he declares.   "Obviously it is
the most difficult and provocative phenomenon of the period
but it has to be fitted into the story, not stand outside it."134

      Jacob, unlike many traditionalists, does not allow an
interest in "psychological consistency" to color his judgment
of all of Richard's actions in the light of the mystery of the
princes.135   Although he rejects More's story of the Tyrell
confession and is not completely convinced by the evidence
of the bones in the Tower,136 he can find no evidence to
prove Richard not guilty.   The fact that the boys disappeared
during Richard's reign and that he took no steps to counter-
act the rumors of their death,137 while not conclusive evi-

dence of his guilt, does tend to lend substance to the accusation.

There can be little question that the most complete and authoritative work on the last Plantagenet king is Paul Murray Kendall's Richard III. This biographical study is based almost entirely on contemporary sources and those bits of the Tudor tradition which can be certified as reliable.[138] No historian can, or should, avoid giving his own interpretation of historical fact, but Kendall refrains, as far as is possible, from the tedious moralizing so common in writers on this subject.

Kendall sees Richard as a complex, uncompromising man caught in a time of change. Tied in many ways to the feudal past, he sought to make his reign "personal, accessible, and paternal."[139] He was, at the same time, aware of the increasing importance and power of the middle classes whose support had been so vital to his brother.[140] His pursuit of justice for the lower classes is evidenced by the many acts in their behalf passed by parliament during this reign as well as by Richard's instructions to royal officials dealing with the treatment of the poor.[141] With penetrating insight Kendall pictures a man caught in a dilemma only partly of his own making.

> Viewed as a social phenomenon, Richard's reign can be seen as an ironic comedy of justice: ironic because he offended against justice in securing the authority by which to pursue it and because his subjects preferred something else, namely, stability. Viewed as the history of a man, his reign shows elements of true tragedy, for the protagonist cannot resolve the conflict within himself and he cannot win his conflict with the world, with which he refuses to compromise.[142]

In Kendall's opinion only three of the many criminal allegations against Richard can be seriously considered in the light of contemporary evidence. The first of these was the execution of Hastings on the charge of treason. Kendall has no doubt that Hastings was indeed conspiring with the Woodvilles against the Protector,[143] but he does not accept the claim made by many of Richard's defenders that Hastings was given a trial and executed a week after his arrest. The execution took place, he declares, immediately after the arrest,[144] an action contrary to Richard's nature and one which

he deeply regretted.[145]   There seems little doubt, Kendall
feels, that most of the council approved the removal of Hastings as necessary for the stability of the government.[146]

Many of Richard's friends, and all of his enemies,
agree that Richard's usurpation of the throne was a criminal
act, although most of the former have attempted to justify it
on grounds of political necessity.   Judgment of this act,
however, must depend, not on the truth of the story of the
pre-contract, but on the question of whether Richard believed
it to be true.   Henry Tudor's attempt to suppress the story,
and his persecution of Stillington lead Kendall to believe that
Richard had good reason to conclude that his brother's children were indeed illegitimate.*   Richard's elevation to the
throne was brought about as much by forces outside his control as by his own ambition.   His election by the Lords and
Commons had some opposition, but most men accepted it as
necessary and even desirable.

The fate of the princes in the Tower is the most controversial and emotion-charged issue of Richard's entire life
and reign.   Because Kendall believes that any discussion of
this question is necessarily speculative and thus has no place
in a biography, he reserves his analysis for an appendix.
There is no proof that Richard murdered his nephews, Kendall states.   That is to say, there is no evidence that would
stand up in a court of law.[148]   No contemporary writer accused Richard of the crime, although there were rumors
spread by the leaders of the Buckingham rebellion that the
boys had met a violent death.[149]   The Tudor version of the
murder, which was based on More's History, has been demonstrated to the satisfaction of most historians, to be completely worthless as legal proof.[150]

Kendall does not reject completely the evidence of
Tanner and Wright in the matter of the bones found in the
Tower.   While their findings are not absolutely conclusive,
Kendall believes that the bones are the remains of the princes

---

*Kendall, Richard III, p. 261.   Levine argues that, even if
there had been a pre-contract between Edward and Eleanor
Butler, the two princes would not have been illegitimate
since Eleanor Butler died in 1468 and the boys were born
in 1470 and 1472 respectively.   The argument is specious
since the death of the first spouse does not legalize a biga-
mous second marriage.   Levine, "Richard III--Usurper or
Lawful King?," p. 391.

and that they were killed in the summer of 1483.   If the
evidence of the bones proves that the boys were killed during Richard's reign, it does not prove that he was responsible. [151]

There are many indications, declares Kendall, that
Richard was not responsible for the death of his nephews.
Among them is the fact that the Croyland chronicler, who
reports the rumor of the death of the princes, does not
accuse Richard of having murdered them. [152]   The behavior
of Elizabeth Woodville in sending her daughters to live at
Richard's court is surely a strong indication that she did not
believe him guilty of the murder of her sons. [153]   The curious wording of the bill of attainder passed against Richard
in Henry Tudor's first parliament, Kendall observes, accusing him in general terms of the shedding of infant blood,
suggests either that Henry knew Richard to be innocent of
the specific murders of the princes, or that his guilt could
not be proved. [154]

After weighing all of the available evidence, Kendall,
like Jacob, comes back to the inescapable fact that the
princes disappeared during Richard's reign and that there is
no evidence that they were ever seen alive afterward.   "This
fact is far more telling than any indications of his guilt that
have been assembled and it weighs heavily against the indications of his innocence which have just been surveyed," he
declares. [155]

If, as Kendall believes likely, the princes died during Richard's reign, could someone other than Richard have
been responsible?   Kendall rejects Markham's case against
Henry Tudor as untenable and considers it unlikely that both
boys died a natural death. [156]   The case against the Duke of
Buckingham, however, cannot be so easily dismissed.
Buckingham had both the opportunity, as Constable of England, and the motive, which was to seize the crown either
for himself or for Henry Tudor.   By murdering the princes
and then blaming Richard for the crime, Buckingham could
gain the support of all of the disaffected elements in the
country. [157]   Indeed, observes Kendall, a great many otherwise unexplainable events become clear if Buckingham, rather than Richard, murdered the princes.   It would explain
how Buckingham was able to assure the rebel leaders that
the boys were dead when, according to More and Vergil,
Richard did not order the murder until several days after
Buckingham left him at Gloucester. [158]   It is unlikely, as

well, that Brackenbury, whom More describes as an honorable man, would have ridden to Bosworth to fight and die for a man who had ordered him to commit the unspeakable crime of murder.[159]

Whoever murdered the princes, whether Richard, Buckingham, Henry Tudor, or persons unknown, the responsibility for their deaths must rest on Richard, Kendall avers.

> Though it seems unlikely that Richard, in deciding to take the crown, realized or was willing to face this fact, his assumption of power contained the death of the Princes within it. Horrible as their fate was, it was not a gratuitous or even an additional deed of violence; the push from the dais was itself the mortal stroke. In this sense it can be said that Richard doomed the Princes. The dark behavior of Henry Tudor, the ambitions and the opportunity possessed by Buckingham, give us reason to doubt, however, that he actually murdered them.[160]

Charles Ross, in his recent biography of Edward IV, places much of the blame for the "unhappy aftermath of his early death" on Edward himself.[161] The king was well aware of the unpopularity of the Woodvilles, Ross declares, yet he not only made no attempt to curb their power, but he gave into their charge his son and heir. The deep divisions between the old and new nobility, the result of Edward's unwise policies, could not possibly be healed by his last-minute attempt to reconcile the warring factions. To Edward must go the doubtful distinction of being the only king in English history since 1066 who failed to secure the safe succession of his son.[162]

Quite obviously, there is little unanimity of opinion among historians on the subject of Richard III. Many writers choose a position and then cite only those facts which tend to support it, ignoring or disputing with dubious logic any evidence which might undermine their case. Others, with greater wisdom and intellectual honesty, examine all the evidence, both negative and positive, before making any judgment. Unlike the absolute verdicts of those who place themselves firmly on one side of the question or the other, the conclusions of the more objective historians tend to be less positive, but unfortunately, almost as speculative.

Six

THE EARLY FICTION

I am determined to prove a villain.
--King Richard III I. i.

If the name Richard III conjurs up any picture in the
minds of millions of people in the English-speaking world,
it is probably safe to assume that the artist who created the
picture was William Shakespeare. Indeed, one need never
have read or seen a performance of King Henry VI,
Part III, or The Tragedy of King Richard III to have
been influenced by them in regard to Richard's appearance
and character. Paul Murray Kendall was quite correct when
he wrote: "While the Tudor chroniclers made up the minds
of subsequent historians about Richard III, Shakespeare has
made up the imagination of everybody else. "[1]

Although Shakespeare may be considered the perfecter
of the Tudor myth in fiction, he was not the first to make
use of the subject. Several earlier poets and playwrights,
using the same sources, had drawn substantially the same
picture. That their efforts were less successful or influential than Shakespeare's may be seen in the fact that they
are little noticed today. These early works are of interest,
however, to anyone who wishes to trace the development of
the Richard III legend in English language fiction over the
past four hundred years.

Two of the earliest known works of fiction relating to
Richard III were probably written late in the reign of Henry
VII or early in the reign of Henry VIII. Both are poems,
or ballads, which were possibly handed down orally for
many years before they were enlarged and put in written
form. Humphrey Brereton, a retainer of Lord Thomas Stanley, is credited as the author of both ballads. [2] "The Song
of the Lady Bessy, " the first of these poems, relates the
involvement of Elizabeth of York (the Lady Bessy of the

73

title) in the plot to overthrow Richard. She asks Lord Stanley to help her write letters in order to raise men to bring
Henry Tudor from Brittany to claim the crown. Stanley
agrees to help Bessy when she tells him that Richard has
asked her to be his lover and has promised to "poison and
put away" both his wife and son. [3] The poem covers a period of about a year, ending with Henry Tudor's victory at
Bosworth and his marriage immediately afterward to the
Lady Bessy.

Apparently, the author had a double purpose in writing
this poem. The first was to show that Elizabeth of York was
the chief organizer and instrument of the conspiracy against
Richard and the second was to show the important role played
by the Stanleys in both the conspiracy and Henry's victory at
Bosworth. [4] The second of these poems, "The Ballad of
Bosworth Field," begins with the summons and arrest of
Stanley's son, Lord Strange, and ends with a description of
the Battle of Bosworth and Henry's crowning. The contribution of the Stanleys to Henry Tudor's success is stressed in
this poem, as in the first.

Both poems contain many anachronisms and errors of
fact. For example, Lord Stanley is several times referred
to as the Earl of Derby, a title he did not receive until the
reign of Henry VII. In "The Song of the Lady Bessy," the
Duke of Norfolk dies fighting for Richard, as, in fact, he
did, [5] but in "The Ballad of Bosworth Field," he is found
fighting for Henry Tudor, Earl of Richmond. [6] Gairdner,
who wrote the notes on these poems, remarked that they contain a great deal of truth which was not easy to separate
from the fantastic additions of the author. [7] Whether one accepts this opinion depends largely on what one regards as
the truth about Richard III. Gairdner's view of the subject
has not been accepted without question by all historians.

A work of much greater literary and historical significance than the two ballads mentioned above is A Mirror
for Magistrates. This collection of verse "tragedies" was
inspired by Lydgate's 1430s translation (the exact date is unknown) of a Boccaccio work about the fall of princes and
John Wayland's Primer, a continuation with additional material about English princes. The first edition of the Mirror
appeared in 1559 and succeeding editions, containing some
revisions as well as additional material, were printed in
1563, 1578, and 1587. Since, in this case, no purpose
would be served by differentiating among the various edi-

tions, they will be treated as a single work. *

The editor of A Mirror for Magistrates was William
Baldwin who, in his address to the reader, declared the
purpose of the work was:

> to have the storye contynewed from where Bochas
> lefte, unto this presente time, chiefly of suche as
> Fortune had dalyed with here in this ylande:
> which might be as a myrrour for al men as well
> noble as others, to shewe the slyppery deceytes
> of the waveryng lady, and the due rewarde of all
> kinde of vice. [8]

Baldwin enlisted the talents of other writers who were to
take as a subject the story of some unfortunate soul whose
experiences could serve as an example to others.   Each of
the tragedies is narrated by the ghost of the person repre-
sented and the subjects were chosen for their value as object lessons rather than for their historical importance.
Frequently historical facts were changed or distorted in order to make a point. [9]   The writers used as their sources
the works of More, Fabyan, and Hall, and the Mirror was,
therefore, in "complete accord with Tudor ideas."[10]

Richard III is the villain in eight of the tragedies in
A Mirror for Magistrates.   In the tragedy entitled "How king
Henry the syxth a vertuous prince, was after many other
miseries cruelly murdered in the Tower of London," Richard is blamed for Henry's murder but not for the death of
Prince Edward.   Speaking to Baldwin, the interlocutor to
whom all of the poems are addressed, Henry declares:

> For there mine only sonne, not thirtene yere of age,
> Was tane and murdered strayte, by Edward in his rage:
> And shortly I my selfe to stymt al furder strife
> Stabbed with his brothers bluddy blade in prison lost
>   my life. [11]

Richard and Edward are also condemned in the tragedy attributed to George Ferrers entitled "How George Plan-

---

*The various editions of the Mirror were progressive and
cumulative.   For example, the first edition contained 19
tragedies, including that of Henry VI.   The second edition
added eight new tragedies, including those of Hastings,
Buckingham, and Jane Shore.

tagenet third sonne of the Duke of Yorke, was by his brother
King Edward wrongfully imprisoned, and by his brother Richard miserably murdered." Clarence, who throughout the
tragedy maintains his innocence of any wrongdoing, claims
that he incurred Edward's anger because of his desire to
marry Mary of Burgundy. Edward falsely accuses and exe-
cutes one of Clarence's servants, and it is Clarence's protest against this unjust act which brings his arrest.[12] There
is no mention made in the poem of Clarence's trial or of
his arrest and execution of his late wife's servant. Because
Richard coveted the crown, Clarence claims, he "forged
tales" to increase Edward's anger and prevent a reconciliation.[13] Still another explanation of these events incorporated
in this tragedy is the frequently told tale to the effect that
Edward sent Clarence to his grave because of a prophesy
that "G" would destroy Edward's children. This version
became a favorite with Tudor partisans who claimed that the
prophesy was fulfilled, but by Richard of Gloucester rather
than by George of Clarence.[14] Clarence's tragedy ends with
his being condemned and imprisoned. With some henchmen,
Richard "(My brother, nay my butcher I may say)" steals
into the Tower, binds his victim, and drowns him in a butt
of malmsey wine.[15]

In the tragedy entitled "How Sir Anthony Wudvile
Lorde Rivers and Skales, Governour of prince Edward, was
with his Nevew Lord Richard Gray and others causeles imprisoned, and cruelly murdered," the author closely followed
More's version of the events surrounding the death of Edward IV. The catalog of Richard's crimes is enlarged upon
in this account, however, for after Richard and the young
king returned to Northampton, Rivers declares:

> There loe duke Richard made hym selfe protector
> Of kyng and realme by open proclamation,
> Though neyther kyng nor Queene were his elector
> Thus he presumed by lawles usurpation.[16]

Still another version of the death of Prince Edward
at Tewkesbury is given in John Dolman's tragedy entitled
"Howe the Lord Hastynges was betrayed by trustyng to much
to his evyl counsayler Catesby, and vilanously murdered in
the tower of London by Richarde Duke of Glocestre." Hastings accuses Edward only of smiting the young prince with
his gauntlet while the actual murder was the work of Clarence, Gloucester, Dorset, and Hastings himself.[17]

The story of the fateful council meeting in the Tower, which Dolman places on June 15 rather than June 13, follows More in most details, including the almost essential strawberry story. * As Richard re-enters the room to make his accusations, his appearance must indeed have struck terror into the hearts of his audience.

> Frownyng he enters, with so chaunged cheare,
> As for myld May had chopped fowle Januere.
> And lowryng on me with the goggle eye,
> The whetted tuske, and furrowed forehead hye,
> His Crooked shoulder bristellyke set up,
> With frothy jaws, whose foame he chawed and suppd,
> With angry lookes that flamed as the fyer. [18]

The "usurpour Boare, that hellyshe freak"[19] makes his accusation of witchcraft, bares his arm and shows his "swynyshe skynne"[20] and Hastings is immediately executed.

"The Complaynt of Henry duke of Buckingham" by Thomas Sackville is considered by many critics to be the only tragedy of real literary merit in the Mirror. In this poem Buckingham explains that he revolted because Richard had murdered his two innocent nephews. [21] Bishop Morton's role is not mentioned and the failure of the revolt is blamed on Buckingham's army of faithless and cowardly commoners. [22]

In the tragedy entitled "Howe Collingbourne was cruelly executed for making a foolishe rime," attributed to Baldwin, the writer of the famous rhyme describes his traitor's death in grisly detail. † He maintains, however, that he meant no harm to the king or his council and that no treason

---

*This incident, related by More (History, p. 47), in which Richard requests some strawberries from Morton's garden at Holborn during the council meeting of June 13, is seen by many writers as one of the little details which give More's narrative the ring of truth. It has been included by almost all writers hostile to Richard since that time.

†Collingbourne's rhyme, which referred to Catesby, Ratcliffe, Lovell, and Richard, ran as follows: "The catte, the ratte, and Lovell our dogge/ Rulyth all England under a hogge." Collingbourne, a former servant of the Duchess of York, was an agent of Henry Tudor, and it was for the crime of treason, rather than versifying, that he was condemned and executed. Kendall, Richard III, pp. 362-363.

was intended or committed.   In explanation of his unjust
punishment he declares:

> But sith the gylty alwayes are suspicious,
> And dread the ruyne that must sewe by reason,
> They can not chose but count theyre counsayle vicious,
> That note theyre faults, and therefore cal it treason. [23]

   Richard's own tragedy, written by Frauncis Seager,
bears the imposing title "How Richard Plantagenet duke of
Gloucester, murdered his brothers children usurping the
crowne, and in the third yeare of his raygne was most
worthely deprived of life and kingdome in Bosworth playne
by Henry Earle of Richemond after called King Henry the
.vii." In his note to the reader which precedes the tragedy,
Seager writes, "For the better understanding whereof, imagine that you see him tormented with Dives in the diepe pit
of Hell, and thence howlinge this that foloweth." [24]   Richard
is pictured as accusing himself of the murders of Clarence,
the two princes, and Buckingham, all of whom stood between
him and the crown.   The account of the death of the princes
follows closely More's version of the event. [25]   Both nobles
and commons turn against the king because of his bloody
deed.   Buckingham revolts to avenge the murders and is
himself captured and unlawfully executed. [26]

   In the prose bridge which precedes Thomas Churchyard's tragedy entitled "Howe Shores wife, Edwarde the
fowerthes concubine, was by king Richarde despoyled of all
her goodes, and forced to do open penance," the author
makes a critical reference to Richard's tragedy.   He declares:

> For it was thought not vehement ynough for so
> violent a man as king Richard had bene.   The
> matter was wel ynough lyked of sum, but the
> meeter was misliked almost of all.   It is not
> meete that so disorderly and unnatural a man as
> kyng Richard was, should observe any metrical
> order in his talke. [27]

The gentle Jane Shore counteracts this unfortunate error
with the violent curses she calls down on her tormentor's
head.

> Oh wicked wombe that such yll fruite did beare,
> Oh cursed earth that yeldeth forth such mud,

The hell consume all things that dyd the good,
The heavens shut theyr gates against thy spryte,
The world tread downe thy glory under feete,

I aske of God a vengeance on thy bones,
Thy stinking corps corrupts the ayre I knowe:
Thy shameful death no earthly wyght bemoans,
For in thy lyfe thy workes were hated so,
That every man dyd wyshe thy overthrowe;
Wherefore I may, though percial nowe I am,
Curse every cause whereof thy body came. [28]

The hand of Sir Thomas More is again evident in Jane's lament about the ingratitude of man. She, who in her happier days had helped so many without asking anything in return, is rebuffed in her hour of misfortune by those she has helped. Much is made in this tragedy, and indeed by most Tudor writers, of the supposition that Richard took all of Jane's goods, and that her penance and imprisonment were imposed for the sole purpose of enabling him to get his hands on her wealth. [29]

In 1610 Richard Niccols published a revised edition of The Mirror for Magistrates. Included were ten new tragedies, all of which were written by Niccols, and which he entitled A Winter Night's Vision. The two Niccols tragedies concerning Richard are entitled "The Lamentable Lives and Deaths of the Two young Princes, Edward the fifth, and his brother Richard Duke of Yorke" and "The Tragical Life and Death of King Richard the Third." The tragedy of the two young princes repeats More's version of events as Niccols describes how the wicked uncle "usurps the crowne, puts both the youths to death,"[30] using Tyrell, Forrest, and Dighton as his instruments.

The portrait of Richard in "The Tragical Life and Death of King Richard the Third" owes more to Shakespeare than to Seager. After describing his unnatural birth Richard declares:

I readie toothed came, as who would say,
Nature by signes unto the world hath show'd
How fiercely he shall bite another day. [31]

This passage is reminiscent of Henry's speech in Act V, scene vi, of Henry VI, Part III, when just before Richard stabs him to death Henry tells him:

Teeth hadst thou in thy head when thou wast born,
To signify thou camst to bite the world.

Richard's monstrous deformity of body and soul is
stressed by Niccols and the sum of his murders has become
larger than the combined accusations in all the earlier tragedies. His victims now include Henry VI and his son Edward,
Rivers, Grey, Vaughn, Hastings, Buckingham, and the two
princes, and finally, his wife, whom he poisons in the hope
that he can marry his niece, Elizabeth. Murder is not
Richard's only crime in Niccols's tragedy. Dr. Shaw had
Richard's consent, according to this version, when, in his
famous sermon he charged the Duchess of York with adultery.

On the night before Bosworth Richard's dreams are
haunted by the ghosts of his victims. His guilty conscience
does not prevent him, however, from fighting bravely on the
following day against the "weake Welch milkesop" and his
army of "rascall French and British runawaies."[32] The
poems ends with Richard's despoiled body being brought to
Leicester for burial.

In 1614, Richard's restless ghost was summoned forth
from Hell once again by the author of a three-part poem entitled "The Ghost of Richard the Third." This work was
written in the manner of the tragedies of A Mirror for Magistrates and has been attributed to Christopher Brooke. The
author claims that he will tell more of the history of Richard III than could be learned from chronicles, plays, or
poems[33] but he quite obviously took his story from Shakespeare's plays. [34]

Part One of the poem, entitled "His Character," describes Richard's birth and childhood. Once again the tale
of Richard's entry into the world, feet first, deformed, complete with teeth, is repeated, including the storms and omens
reported by Shakespeare. Richard's ghost declares that at
seeing him:

Th'amazed women started; for each jaw
Appear'd with teeth: which mark made these ils good,
That I should woory soules, suck humane blood. [35]

This awful prophesy is quickly fulfilled, for even as
a child Brooke's Richard is a monster of depravity. In re-
calling his childhood Richard declares:

In progress of my childhood, with delight
I taught my nature to see fowles to bleede;
Then, at the slaughter-house, with hungry sight,
Upon slaine beasts my sensuall part did feede;
And (that which gentler natures might affright)
I search't their entrayles, as in them to reade
(Like th'ancient bards) what fate should thence betide,
To cherish sin and propagate my pride. 36

To learn to conquer pity, if indeed Brooke can believe that
Richard had ever experienced that soft emotion, he attended
court sessions, watched as men were condemned to death,
and then attended the executions. This part of his childhood
Richard recalls fondly as "my cordiall and my nourishing
food."37

Part Two of the poem, "The Legend of Richard the
Third," opens with a paean of praise to Shakespeare, in
which Richard's ghost promises to fill in any gaps which the
Bard may have left in his story. 38 He then recounts the
litany of his crimes, including all of the murders for which
he was blamed by earlier writers, and the calumny which
he caused to be spread against his mother's good name.
Since Edward's children had also been declared bastards in
Shaw's sermon, Richard confesses:

Thus father, mother, brother, race and name,
I would have vilify'd t'advance my claime. 39

In Part Three, "The Tragedie of Richard the Third,"
Richard's conscience at last begins to bother him. Indeed,
he is so overwhelmed by the enormity of his crimes that he
falls into melancholic despair. He lives in the dread certainty of his punishment to come, for there is no expiation
for sins such as his. He exclaims:

I sorrow'd desperately, because my sorrow
Was all too late to helpe my helplesse plight. 40

The peers and commons rise against him and join the ranks
of Richmond. In desperation, Richard summons the poor,
ragged, half-starved men of the north to come to his aid.
They respond in the hope of being fed, rather than out of
any love for the king. Indeed, the soldiers in his entire
army

> All sought to loose rather then win the day,
> And seem'd more Richmond's part than friends
>   of myne. [41]

With soldiers such as these, the outcome was inevitable.
Richmond, having on his side a loyal army and the blessings
of heaven, won the day and the crown.   The result, Brooke
declares, was a happy one.

> Now England's chaos was reduc't to order
> By god-like Richmond. [42]

Interest in the life and death of the last Plantagenet
was not limited, during the sixteenth and seventeenth centuries, to writers of didactic poetry.   The dramatic possi-
bilities of the story of the wicked usurper and his pathetic
victims appealed strongly to playwrights as well.   Indeed,
what is probably the first historical play printed in English
was entitled The True Tragedie of Richard the Third. [43]
The author of this one-act play, which was published in 1594,
is unknown.   The play itself is badly written, part of the
dialogue being in meter and part in prose, and the historical
facts, even by the standards of the times, are grossly distorted.   Richard Grey has become Elizabeth Woodville's
brother and his arrest and execution resulted from his having
taken money from the Tower to give to England's Scottish
enemies. [44]   Pierre Landois, the Breton who did all in his
power to deliver Henry Tudor into Richard's hands, in this
play accompanies Tudor to England to help him win the
crown. [45]

Most of the characters and incidents are, however,
depressingly familiar, and the influence of Sir Thomas More
is evident throughout the play.   Richard is

> A man ill shaped, crooked backed, lame armed, withall,
> Valiantly minded, but tyrannous in authoritie. [46]

He commits all of the frequently recounted murders and, at
Bosworth Field is slain by Richmond himself, [47] who tells
his troops:

> Because I will be foremost in this fight,
> To incounter with that bloodie murtherer,
> My self will lead the vaward of our troop. [48]

The play ends with an Epilogue, aptly described by the play's

nineteenth-century editor as "preposterous,"[49] in which a
chorus of messengers, joined by Elizabeth of York and
Elizabeth Woodville, recall the glory and wisdom of each
of the Tudor monarchs.

Obviously, this play holds little interest for the stu-
dent of either history or literature, except for the fact of
its having been written before any of Shakespeare's plays in
which Richard appeared.   There is, in fact, strong evidence
to support the belief that Shakespeare was familiar with this
tragedy.   There are striking similarities of dialogue in
Shakespeare's Richard the Third and the True Tragedy, no-
tably in the Tower when Hastings is arrested and executed,
and the final scenes depicting the battle at Bosworth.   This
is merely another of the far from rare examples in the history of literature in which a genius took someone else's
ideas and made of them something far more memorable than
the original.

King Edward the Fourth, Part II, by the actor-author
Thomas Heywood is still another late-sixteenth-century play
which draws heavily on the Tudor chronicles and Sir Thomas
More, as well as on popular ballads for its characterization
of Richard III.   It was written probably around 1594 and was
printed in 1600, and reprinted in 1619 and 1626.   Heywood's
Richard was, as one critic wrote, "a very vulgar villain."[50]
He announces to the audience early in the play, "I am a
true-stampt villain as ever lived,"[51] and then procedes to
perpetrate, in the course of a few days, all of the crimes
which other writers had accused him of committing between
1478 and 1483.

Clarence is the first victim.   Dr. Shaw, at Richard's
direction, convinces Edward that the G who according to the
prophesy would kill his children is George of Clarence.
There are to be no surprises in the play, for Richard declares his intention to the audience.

> Ha! the mark thou aim'st at, Richard, is a crown,
> And many stand betwixt thee and the same.
> What of all that?   Doctor, play thou thy part:
> I'll climb up by degrees, through many a heart. [52]

The next victims are the two little princes who are
murdered in the Tower on the very night they are imprisoned
there.   Brackenbury, the Constable of the Tower, resigns
his post in revulsion at the murders of the children and also

Richard's treatment of Jane Shore.   Jane is truly the pathetic
heroine of this play.   This kind, loyal, warmhearted lady is
persecuted by the Protector who, after stripping her of all
of her possessions, turns her out into the streets to beg for
her livelihood, forbidding any man, on pain of death, to help
her in any way.   Mistress Shore quite naturally finds Richard's cruel treatment surprising since, as she tells a friend,
in former days she had helped him when he begged for help,
and had even interceded with Edward on his behalf. [53]   Jane
expires, presumably as a result of this harsh treatment, in
the arms of her estranged husband.

          In act five of this tragedy, Richard is finally crowned.
Immediately after the coronation, Buckingham offers the new
king a bride--Anne of Warwick.   Richard accepts this offer,
but rejects Buckingham's request for the lands of the Earl
of Hereford.   Angry at this snub, Buckingham vows to bring
Harry Richmond to England and place him on the throne.

          Quite obviously, Heywood gave his imagination free
reign in his treatment of history.   Despite this not uncom-
mon failing of writers of historical fiction, in the twentieth
as well as the sixteenth century, this play is important
enough to merit some attention.

          Certainly Shakespeare's Richard III is no less a cari-
cature than the man portrayed in the works already discussed, yet after nearly four hundred years he is, to most
people, a historical reality.   Indeed, the playwright's reputation as a historian has been so widely accepted that the
first Duke of Marlborough allegedly declared that Shakespeare
was the only history he ever read, [54] and all too many since
that time might make the same admission.   Shakespeare took
the chronicles of Hall and Holinshed, transformed them with
his own genius and imagination, and produced a villain un-
equalled in theatrical literature.   The three plays written by
or attributed to Shakespeare, in which Richard III appears,
may indeed be great drama, but they cannot truthfully be
called history.

          Richard makes his first, brief appearance in The
Second Part of King Henry VI, first printed in 1594 under
the title The First Part of the Contention of the Two Famous
Houses of Yorke and Lancaster.   The authorship of this play
has been the subject of much dispute among Shakespearean
scholars.   The original play has been attributed variously to
Marlowe, Peele, Greene, and Shakespeare, in differing

combinations, but the revised version as printed in 1594 is generally believed to be the work of Shakespeare. [55]

Richard's character is more fully developed in The Third Part of King Henry the Sixth, the last play in the trilogy.   Like the second part, the authorship of the third part has been attributed to various authors, including Shakespeare, but his sole authorship is generally accepted by scholars. [56]

In The Tragedy of King Richard III Shakespeare leads Richard along his bloody, corpse-strewn path to the throne and finally, to his inevitable and well-deserved end on Bosworth Field.   This play, which was written probably in 1593, [57] draws quite heavily on Holinshed's Chronicles and More's History, and shows some evidence of the author's familiarity with The True Tragedy of Richard the Third. [58]

There are many examples of anachronisms and distortions of fact to be found in these three plays.   A few will suffice to illustrate the point.   Richard's brief appearance in Henry VI, part two, occurs during the first Battle of St. Albans which took place in 1455.   Richard, who was actually a child of three at the time, is pictured as slaying Somerset. In the opening scene of Henry VI, part three, he carries his victim's head in triumph to parliament.   In this play, Shakespeare places Richard at the battle of Mortimer's Cross and Towton. [59]   At the time these battles took place, Richard was eight years old and living in Burgundy under the protection of Duke Philip.

Shakespeare's description of Richard's physical and emotional deformity, which was destined to become an important aspect of the Tudor myth, is repeated by several of the characters in each of the three plays.   Before the Battle of St. Albans, Clifford taunts Richard with these words:

Hence, heap of wrath, foul indigested lump,
As crooked in thy manners as thy shape! [60]

Shakespeare seems to have considered the description apt enough to bear repeating, for Henry VI addresses Richard as an "indigested and deformed lump," [61] and Anne Neville calls him "Thou lump of foul deformity." [62]   Richard's description of himself is no more flattering.   He is, he declares:

> Deform'd, unfinished, sent before my time
> Into this breathing world, scarce half made up,
> And that so lamely and unfashionable
> That dogs bark at me as I halt by them. [63]

Richard's bodily deformity is matched by his warped nature. Too monstrous to be loved, he vows to compensate for his withered arm, humped back, and misshapen legs, by seizing the crown. [64] Several people who stand in his way fall victim to his ambitions. After the battle of Tewkesbury, the three sons of York stab Prince Edward of Lancaster to death and Richard attempts to kill the prince's mother as well. Foiled in this attempt, he hastens to London where Henry VI is imprisoned in the Tower. [65] The saintly king, knowing he is doomed, describes to Richard his strange and unnatural birth and repulsive appearance. Richard thereupon stabs Henry to death, declaring:

> Then, since the heavens have shaped my body so,
> Let hell make crook'd my mind to answer it. [66]

The villain then gives his audience a hint of events to come. He announces:

> King Henry and the prince his son are gone:
> Clarence, thy turn is next, and then the rest. [67]

In the last of the three plays, Richard plots the destruction of Clarence by attempting to convince Edward that the G prophesied to kill his children is George of Clarence. Richard confesses that he has murdered Henry VI, his son Edward, and Warwick, whose daughter Anne he now intends to wed. [68] Richard hires two assassins to murder Clarence, intending to place the blame on the queen and her family. He can then pretend to avenge Clarence's murder by executing Rivers, Vaughn, and Grey, thus eliminating several more obstacles in his path to the throne. [69]

Shakespeare follows the traditional Tudor version of Richard's slanderous attack on the legitimacy of his brothers [70] and repeats More's error by naming Elizabeth Lucy as the lady with whom Edward made the pre-contract. [71] More's version of the death of the princes, which was accepted almost unanimously by Tudor writers, is followed quite closely in this play. After his coronation, Richard complains to Buckingham that the boys are still alive.

Shall I be plain? I wish the bastards dead;
And I would have it suddenly perform'd. [72]

Tyrell is the instrument of the princes' death and, this deed
accomplished, Richard turns his attention to his next victim.
He tells Catesby to spread rumors to the effect that Anne is
mortally ill for, although she is his wife, she has outlived
her usefulness.   Richard declares:

I must be married to my brother's daughter,
Or else my kingdom stands on brittle glass.
Murder her brothers, and then marry her! [73]

Buckingham rebels against Richard because of the murder of
the princes and Richard's refusal to honor his promise to
turn over the Hereford inheritance. [74]   Thus Richard loses
his last supporter and his alienation is complete.

On the night before Bosworth the ghosts of Richard's
victims come to haunt him and to wish Richmond success in
the coming battle. It must be assumed that Richmond's victory was pre-ordained, as Buckingham tells him that "God
and good angels fight on Richmond's side." [75]   Richard wakes
in a sweat of fear, realizing too late the cost of his ambition.   "There is no creature loves me;/ And if I die, no
soul will pity me," he laments. [76]   This can surely have
been no startling revelation to Richard since his own mother
had found it impossible to love him.   "Take with thee my
most heavy curse," she has told him. [77]

The contrast, so frequently stressed by Tudor writers,
between Richard, the embodiment of evil, and Henry Tudor,
his god-like successor, was not overlooked by Shakespeare.
Before the Battle of Bosworth, Henry describes to his troops
the man they must defeat.

Truly, gentlemen, a bloody tyrant and a homicide;
One raised in blood, and one in blood establish'd:
One that made means to come by what he hath,
And slaughter'd those that were the means to help him;
A base foul stone, made precious by the foil
Of England's chair, where he is falsely set;
One that hath ever been God's enemy. [78]

Compare this with Henry VI's address to Henry Tudor, then
the young Earl of Richmond.

> Come hither, England's hope. If secret powers
> Suggest but truth to my divining thoughts,
> This pretty lad will prove our country's bliss.
> His looks are full of peaceful majesty,
> His head by nature framed to wear a crown,
> His hand to wield a sceptre, and himself
> Likely in time to bless a regal throne. [79]

In Shakespeare's typically Tudor view, the battlefield of Bosworth was the scene of mortal combat between God's instrument and God's enemy. Richard was slain and Henry Tudor took his rightful place as England's king. [80]

Ben Jonson, a contemporary and friend of Shakespeare, used Richard III as the subject of his play Richard Crookback, which he wrote in 1602, and which was probably performed regularly for several years. [81] Unfortunately, this play is no longer extant, but it is probably safe to assume that Jonson used the same sources and drew the same conclusions about Richard as did his contemporaries.

The legend was perpetuated, if not embellished, by writers of the Stuart period, whose monarchs derived their claim to the throne from the Tudors. In 1629, Sir John Beaumont's Bosworth Field: With a Taste of the Variety of Other Poems was edited and published posthumously by his son. In accordance with the father's wishes, the work was dedicated to the king. [82] Indeed, the apparent purpose of the title poem was to glorify the Stuarts. The many digressions from the main subject, in which the author praises monarchs who ruled more than a century after the Battle of Bosworth, seem forced and out of place. For example, in his description of the battle, Beaumont tells of the bravery of Bernard, a lord of Scotland and "a blossom of the Stuarts happy line, which is on Brittaines throne ordain'd to shine."[83]

The poet begins by describing the events of the night before the battle. Richard, awakened from dreams in which he has been haunted by the ghosts of his victims, dons his armor and goes out to inspect his camp. He comes upon a sleeping sentry and, in a rage, he stabs the man to death. [84]

Meanwhile, in his camp, the sleeping Richmond is visited in his dreams by an angel who urges him to fight to win the crown. The angel assures Richmond that "the heav'n shall blesse thy hopes, and crowne thy joyes."[85] The heavenly messenger then shows Henry a glorious throne

on which a king is seated, like a "bright Apollo." This
vision is the "wise and potent James" who has ended the
border wars and joined England and Scotland. [86]

At the height of the battle Richard, failing to realize
that Richmond is as brave as his Scottish followers and his
Stuart descendants, charges toward him. He slays Brandon
and Cheney and then discovers how mistaken he was in think-
ing Richmond a coward.

> Alas? how much deceiv'd, when he shall find
> An able body and courageous mind:
> For Richmond boldly doth himselfe oppose
> Against the King, and gives him blowes for blowes,
> Who now confesseth with an angry frowne,
> His Rivall, not unworthy of the Crowne. [87]

But, even had Stanley's treachery not turned the tide against
him, Richard was doomed, for God was fighting on the other
side.

> But that great God, to whom all creatures yeeld,
> Protects his servant with a heav'nly shield,
> His pow'r, in which the Earle securely trusts,
> Rebates the blowes, and falsifies the thrusts. [88]

The unequal fight, and the poem, end as Richard is slain by
Richmond.

On March 7, 1667, Samuel Pepys noted in his diary
a visit to the Duke of York's playhouse where he saw "'The
English Princesse, or Richard the Third'; a most sad,
melancholy play, and pretty good; but nothing eminent in it,
as some tragedys are. "[89] The full title of this play which
Pepys found moving if undistinguished, is The English
Princesse, or The Death of Richard the III. It was written
by John Caryll in 1666 and published in 1667, and the Prologue gives evidence that writers well into the Stuart period
still looked to the Tudor chroniclers as their source of information about Richard III.

> But to plain Hollinshed and down-right Stow
> We the coarse Web of our Contrivance owe. [90]

Actually, Caryll owed as much to his imagination as to
Hollinshed and Stow. His Richard is the standard Tudor
monster, but several rather curious additions have been
made to the familiar tale.

   The plot concerns Richard's determination to marry
his niece, Elizabeth, and her bitter opposition to the proposal. Richard's scheme has the support of Elizabeth Woodville who reasons that, since the king's safety depends on
this marriage, he would be forced to protect both his queen
and her family. To this argument her daughter replies:

> Shall then the Butcher of our Familie
> By me, and by my love protected be?[91]

Further arguments to the effect that Elizabeth must either
marry Richard or be destroyed by him are to no avail. It
is not only her hatred of Richard, but also her love for Henry Tudor that make the princess so adamant in her refusal
of her uncle's proposal. She declares:

> A Mother, and a Tyrant joyn to force
> My plighted heart to an unjust Divorce:
> But, Richmond! the Temptation of a Crown
> Shall not divert me, nor a Tyrant's frown:
> I'll follow thee, whom powerful Heaven does lead
> To save the living, and revenge the Dead. [92]

   The popular princess has captured the heart of a
third suitor and would-be king. William Stanley, the step-
uncle of Henry Tudor, has decided that the happiest solution
of the conflict between York and Lancaster would be for
Richard and Richmond to destroy each other, leaving possession of both Elizabeth and the crown to him. Henry
Tudor, however, does not desire the crown for himself.
Lord Thomas Stanley shows Elizabeth a letter from Henry
in which he promises to restore the crown to her, or die
in the attempt. [93] Inspired by Richmond's certainty of success, Elizabeth is able to withstand Richard's threat that she
must marry him or die. [94]

   Richmond receives encouragement from another,
rather unexpected source. The Priour of Litchfield informs
him of a prophesy written centuries earlier by Gildas, in
which the struggle between Richard and Richmond and its
outcome are foretold. According to Gildas:

> the fury of a Savage Boar
> Shall his own Blood, and then this Land devour.
> Then he describes the Man, (and you are he)
> Who must redeem this Realm from Tyrannie;
> Who after Conquest shall by force of Love

More then by War, our happiness improve.
For peaceful England shall the Roses find
No more in battel, but in marriage joyn'd. [95]

While Richard remains on the throne, however, Elizabeth is in great danger. To prevent her marriage to Henry, Richard hires Forrest to murder her, as he has murdered her brothers. Richmond comes to save her life, or to die with her, but, arguing that he must be ruled by reason rather than passion, Elizabeth persuades him to return to his troops.

The scene on the night before Bosworth, in which Richard is haunted by the ghosts of his victims, follows the Tudor tradition closely, and there are only minor variations in the battle scenes themselves. By the time the play was written, it had become an established part of the myth that Henry Tudor had killed Richard in single-handed combat, and Caryll uses this dramatic scene as the climax of his play. In the final moments of the drama, the victorious Richmond has to be persuaded to wear the crown. He insists that it belongs rightfully to Elizabeth, but he finally yields to her argument that since he earned the crown he deserved to wear it. [96]

The Epilogue of the play is addressed to Henry Tudor, but aimed, quite obviously, at Charles II. The author admonishes the monarch:

Richard is dead; and now begins your reign:
Let not the Tyrant live in you again.
For though one Tyrant be a nation's Curse,
Yet Commonwealths of Tyrants are much worse.
Their Name is Legion; and a Rump (you know)
In Cruelty all Richards does outgo.

Richard III, as portrayed by the poets and playwrights of the sixteenth and seventeenth centuries, came straight from the pages of the early Tudor chronicles and the History of Sir Thomas More. It is not at all surprising that this version of the man and his history was accepted without question as readily by writers of fiction as it was by early historians. The fact that Richard evolved into an impossibly depraved and evil monster did not result in rejection of this almost ludicrous caricature, but served rather to make the character more memorable. One cannot call the sixteenth and seventeenth centuries a historically critical age. As the study of history developed and changed, however, so too did the views of many writers of fiction regarding Richard III.

Seven

THE LATER FICTION

For slander lives upon succession,
For ever housed where it gets possession.
--The Comedy of Errors III, i.

After the Stuart period interest in Richard apparently
waned, and more than a century and a half was to pass before he again attracted the attention of writers of fiction.
By that time the novel had become established. This was a
new literary form which allowed an author greater scope
than either poetry or drama for the development of both plot
and character. Sir Walter Scott popularized the use of historical events as the background of the novel,* and many
other writers followed his lead.

The success or failure of historical novels depends,
quite naturally, on the author's willingness to research his
subject thoroughly, as well as on his talent as a writer.
Some novelists who chose to write about Richard III and his
period seemed quite content to read More's History and the
plays of Shakespeare in order to acquire what appeared to
them sufficient knowledge of the subject. Others, determined
to capture the flavor of the period and achieve historical accuracy, delved much deeper into chronicles, records, and
narrative histories.

The earliest of the novels in which Richard plays a
significant role is Edward Bulwer-Lytton's The Last of the
Barons, published in 1843. Warwick, the baron referred to
in the title, is the hero of this work, which is strongly Lancastrian and anti-Yorkist in tone. The earl is portrayed as
the noblest, most unselfish, and bravest man of his time,

---

*Two of Scott's novels dealing with this period, Quentin Dur-
ward (1823) and Anne of Geierstein (1829) take place mainly
on the continent and are therefore of only secondary interest
here.

and his well-known and overriding ambition and arrogance
are ignored, or denied, by the author. In this novel Warwick appears as a man whose virtues have made him the
most popular baron in England while the shifty, untrustworthy,
Woodville-dominated Edward IV has become the most unpopular.

Warwick's disenchantment with Edward begins soon
after the Woodville marriage, but he remains loyal in the
hope that under the Neville influence the king can be guided
along the path of virtue. When Edward attempts to seduce
Anne Neville, however, her father realizes that the honor
and prosperity of both England and the Nevilles can be restored only under the Lancastrians.[1] He decides to play the
kingmaker once more.

Anne Neville, unlike her father, has been a lifelong
Lancastrian. She has been in love with Edward of Lancaster
since childhood and her only desire is to see him wrest the
crown from the usurping Edward of York.[2] Warwick's reconciliation with Margaret of Anjou appears to put both young
Edward and the crown within Anne's reach.

Unfortunately for the Lancastrians, the Yorkist cause
is ably served by Machiavellian Richard of Gloucester, the
"crafty pigmy" whose loyalty to Edward during his lifetime
is unquestioned by Bulwer-Lytton.[3] Richard's subtle, crafty
nature is illustrated by his suggestion that Edward offer his
daughter Elizabeth as the bride of Edward of Lancaster in
order to forestall the reconciliation between Warwick and
Margaret of Anjou.[4] Indeed, Richard is credited with having
initiated most of Edward's rather underhanded domestic and
foreign policies.

At the Battle of Barnet, Warwick orders his troops to
spare the commons, while Edward, on the other hand, tells
his men, "I say to you Slay All!"[5] The author claims Hall's
Chronicle as the authority for this incident,[6] and this is only
one of several instances in which he distorts the facts in
order to make his point. Hall makes no mention of Warwick's instructions to his army in regard to the fate of the
commons and he declares merely that, contrary to his usual
custom, Edward did not order that the commons who had
chosen to fight for Warwick be spared.[7]

Both of the contending armies at Barnet fight coura-
geously, but it is the almost inhuman bravery of Richard of

Gloucester that turns the tide of victory for the Yorkists.
Strangely attired in a blood-red cape over his armor, he
screams war cries and encourages his men with predictions
of the dire fate in store for the enemy.   There was, says
the author, "something ghastly and preternatural" in the
"fiend-like" Richard, who seemed to be everywhere on the
battlefield at once. [8] He engages Warwick in hand-to-hand
combat but the earl escapes to meet his death at other
hands. [9]

  In London, after their victory, the royal brothers are
reunited with the queen and her infant son.   Catching the
"glittering and fatal eye" of the Duke of Gloucester, the
queen holds her child closer, as if she knows instinctively
that he will one day be destroyed by the ruthless ambition
of his uncle. [10]

  Bulwer-Lytton saw the Wars of the Roses as a struggle between the urban middle class and the feudal aristocracy.   He lamented the fact the men engaged in commerce,
"the true spirit of the age, fought for the false Edward, and
against the honest earl." [11] He accepted, subject to his own
interpretation, the views of both the Tudor and the traditional nineteenth-century historians in regard to Richard, but he
was a Lancastrian, not a Tudor, in spirit.   Indeed, he accuses the Tudors of using the middle classes to destroy the
feudal aristocracy in order to establish an absolute monarchy
under an arbitrary tryant. [12]   The author's unrealistic view
of the characters of whom he writes, and his excessively
florid narrative and dialogue, make this novel an example of
Victorian romanticism at its worst.

  In 1849, only a few years after the appearance of
The Last of the Barons, G. P. R. James published The
Woodman; A Romance of the Times of Richard III.   The setting is indeed the fifteenth century, but the characters are
nineteenth century.   The ladies are pure, virtuous, beautiful, and Protestant, and the gentlemen noble, gallant, and
Protestant.   The story abounds in plots, sub-plots, hidden
identities, and long-lost relatives, and James's style is as
floridly romantic as Bulwer-Lytton's.   The tone of this
novel is also Lancastrian, rather than Tudor, but James,
though critical of Richard, is quite moderate in his treatment of him.

  The Richard of this novel represents a radical change
from the hunchbacked monster of earlier centuries.   James
sees him as a man whose:

features were delicate and beautiful, the eyes dark,
keen and expressive.... One shoulder was rather
higher than the other, but not so much as to be a
striking deformity; and the left arm seemed somewhat smaller than its fellow. No means had been
taken to conceal these defects; and yet he might
have passed anywhere for an exceedingly good-looking man, had it not been for a certain expression
of fierce and fiery passion which occasionally came
into his countenance, blending strangely with the
look of sarcastic acuteness which it usually wore.[13]

Good-looking he may have been, but Richard is nonetheless a villain. Although the death of Anne, whom Richard
loved, is attributed to grief over the loss of her son, her
widower is planning an immediate marriage with his niece
Elizabeth, a girl young and healthy enough to produce heirs
to the throne.[14] Richard is not acquitted, however, of the
murders of the princes. Bishop Morton says, in justification of his support of Henry Tudor's claim, "Better a cold
and greedy prince upon the throne, than a murdering usurper."[15] If the picture of Richard has changed a great deal
since Tudor times, so indeed has that of Henry who is no
longer regarded as "England's hope" and God's chosen ruler
of England.

Although G. P. R. James believes Richard to have
been guilty of several crimes, including the murder of the
princes, he disputes the truth of much of the Tudor legend.
It was, he claims, the news of Richmond's invasion which
turned the people of England against the king, in great measure because of the propaganda which attended the invasion.

Every evil act which Richard had committed was
called to memory, denounced, and exaggerated.
False facts were fabricated, many of which have
been transmitted to the present day, to blacken
his conduct. His views, his deeds, his very person were all distorted; and the current of popular
opinion was turned strongly against him.[16]

This note of moderation struck by an anti-Ricardian author
would have been unacceptable, if not actually dangerous,
during the Tudor period, and was indeed a rarity even in
the nineteenth and twentieth centuries.

Richard, as Duke of Gloucester, makes a brief appearance in Robert Louis Stevenson's <u>The Black Arrow</u>, a novel published in 1888. The story, which follows the adventures of a young adherent of the House of York, takes place probably in 1461, as indicated by a footnote which informs the reader that Richard would actually have been far too young at the time to be in command of a part of his brother's army.[17] Since Stevenson indicates merely that the story takes place during the Wars of the Roses, the date could well be 1471. The young hero saves Gloucester's life and is rewarded with knighthood, an honor he is reluctant to accept from "the bold, black-hearted, and ambitious hunchback."[18] Stevenson, though Yorkist in sympathy, still accepted the Tudor portrayal of Richard.

An entirely different view of Richard was presented by novelist John Reed Scott in <u>Beatrix of Clare</u>, published in 1907. This book suffers from some of the same faults as those noted in the Bulwer-Lytton and James novels, but it is nonetheless an interesting and well-written work. Those liberties which the author took with historical fact were to enable him to dramatize a scene, such as Rivers's attempt, after his arrest, to send messengers to Stony Stratford.[19]

The action of the story takes place in the period between the death of Edward IV and the execution of Buckingham. Richard is portrayed throughout as a good, kind man, and a stern, but just king. Perhaps the most interesting aspect of this novel is the author's explanation of the fate of the two little princes. Sir Robert Brackenbury, as Constable of the Tower, had the boys in his charge. He reports to Richard the terrible news.

> [Brackenbury] 'In the morning I found them dead--
>   in each breast a grievous wound--Edward's
>   bloody dagger on the floor.'
>
> [Richard] 'And your view of it?'
>
> [Brackenbury] 'That Edward killed Richard and
>   himself. He had lately been oppressed with
>   heavy melancholy.'
>
> [Richard] 'Yes, that is doubtless the solution.
>   Yet scant credence will be given it. To the
>   kingdom it will be murder foul.'[20]

Richard decides to conceal the murder-suicide because he knows he will be blamed. Of all the solutions offered to ex-

plain the fate of the princes, this must rank as one of the
most ingenious.

Richard received favorable treatment in another early
twentieth-century novel, The Confession of Richard Plantagenet. The author, Dora Greenwell McChesney, was an American who spent most of her life in England as an ardent
champion of unpopular causes. 21   Several of her romantic
novels dealt with Prince Rupert and other Royalists of the
Civil War.   McChesney's interest in Richard came late in
her short life, and this novel was left incomplete at the time
of her death in 1912.   Several unfinished chapters were
omitted, and the rest of the book was tied together and published posthumously by L. Maye, one of the author's friends.

The novel is well researched, a fact the reader is
asked to bear in mind since Richard's character does not
coincide with the traditional view. 22   In regard to his physical appearance, however, some aspects of the Tudor influence persist.   Richard's face has a "subtle beauty" but his
body is misshapen and he walks with a limp. 23

McChesney sees Richard as a man doomed from birth.
A visionary warns him, "Hath not God signed thee, scape-
goat and sacrifice? ... [I]n thee shall thy house answer
for its sins, and in thee be crowned and smitten. "24

Not all the sins are committed by other members of
the House of York.   Richard must bear responsibility for
several of his own.   On the field of Tewkesbury he deliberately kills Edward of Lancaster, his rival for the hand of
Anne Neville. 25   A few days later, when Henry learns from
the guilty man himself how Edward met his death, he dies
of "melancholy and displeasure. "26

When Clarence is sentenced to death, Richard inter-
cedes on his behalf, but only for his mother's sake.   In his
heart he feels that Clarence must die, for should Edward die
leaving a minor heir, Clarence would be a danger to Richard.
Edward rejects Richard's insincere pleas to spare Clarence's
life, but he does give him a warrant to carry out a private
execution.   In the Tower, Richard poisons a goblet of malmsey wine and urges his brother to drink it to spare the family
much pain and embarrassment.   When Clarence refuses to
commit suicide, Richard forces him to drink the poisoned
wine. 27

After Edward's death Richard is determined to remain
loyal to his young nephew, despite his secret, lifelong desire
to be king and his councillors' insistence that he seize the
crown.   Although he had known the secret of the pre-contract even before Edward's death he refuses, at this point,
to make use of it. [28]   When he learns, however, that Edward
had attempted to seduce Anne, Richard decides that neither
Edward nor his son has any further claim on his loyalty,
and he determines to take the crown. [29]

Although he usurps the throne, Richard is innocent
of the deaths of his nephews.   The boys were murdered by
Catesby, acting on instructions from Buckingham who feels
they are a danger to Richard.   Richard is horrified when he
learns of the deed, but realizing that he has been the unwit-
ting and unwilling cause of the murders, he accepts the
blame.   He realizes as well, however, that the deaths of
the princes must be kept secret, for, however innocent of
the crime he may be, all men would judge him guilty. [30]

Richard takes the position and responsibilities of the
kingship very seriously.   He prays to live long enough to
make England strong and peaceful, but it was not only his
desire to give his country good government that led him to
seize the crown.   He knew that he was hated by the Woodvilles and betrayed by Hastings, and he feared for his life
should they control the young king.   He confesses that these
were the reasons that he broke his oath of loyalty to Edward V.

> I doubted could I hold my own, and, if I fell,
> with me fell all things.   What had chanced to
> Thomas of Gloucester and Humfrey of Gloucester,
> Protectors of Kings?   I that bore their title, I
> feared their fate--to die by violence untimely ere
> my work was done! [31]

Woven into this sympathetic portrait of Richard are
traits and incidents that have their origin in the Tudor
legends which the author seemed intent on discrediting.
Those parts of the tradition which this author accepted,
however, such as the murders of Edward of Lancaster and
Clarence, are explained on rather a more human and ra-
tional level than can be found in any of the sixteenth- or
seventeenth-century works.

Carola Oman prefaced her novel, Crouchback, with
the inscription:

> Here is the Book of Crouchback, being the true
> chronicle of that most valiant prince of evil mem-
> ory, King Richard the Third of Old England, a
> man born within this realm, very lord and master
> of it in his own day, and to this hour sole master
> of his own secret and subtle heart. [32]

In this work, the Richard of the Tudor myth reappears,
minus the hump and withered arm. He is brave, cold, in-
secure, and probably murderous, although the implication is
that he murdered only the two young princes. Despite the
title and preface, this is really the story of Anne Neville
and her relationships with other members of her family,
and Richard remains a shadowy figure throughout. The book
is very well written and researched, as befits the daughter
of a famous and distinguished historian, but the reader is
left to wonder what this author really felt about her title
character.

There is nothing that is either shadowy or equivocal
in the portrait of Richard in Patrick Carleton's excellent
novel, Under the Hog, published in 1938. He presents a
vivid and detailed picture of the life and the characters of
the period, and his accurate descriptions of the important
events make this novel almost a narrative history.

To portray historical figures in a novel without
making them wooden and unrealistic is at best a difficult
undertaking, but Carleton manages to escape that pitfall.
His Richard is neither saint nor monster, but rather a withdrawn, cool, clever loner with a code of behavior to which
he adheres at all costs. In attempting to explain this code
to Anne Neville he says, "I tell you that when I choose what
I think to be right I'll stop at no wrong to accomplish it. "[33]

Richard's actions after Buckingham's rebellion ex-
emplify his philosophy. He orders the death of the princes
to prevent a rising in their names and a continuation of the
bloody civil war. [34] Carleton accounts Richard innocent,
however, of all of the other murders of which he has been
accused, and, on balance, Richard emerges as the most at-
tractive and honorable member of the House of York or its
adherents.

Richard is found "not guilty" of the murders of the
princes in Marian Palmer's well-written novel, The White
Boar. The author portrays him as a basically good but

driven man.   Fear of the Woodvilles and the loss of his only
son forced him to take measures against his true nature.   As
Lord of the North, he was firm, but always fair; as king,
he was frequently harsh, as, for example, in his punishment
of Colingbourne. [35]

Palmer, like McChesney before her, blames the death
of the princes on Buckingham, using Tyrell rather than
Catesby as his instrument, and she, too, has Richard accept
the blame for the crime. [36]   On the night before Bosworth he
tells Philip Lovell, a cousin of Francis Lovell and a leading
character in the novel:

> I have done evil in my life of my own will, and
> more has followed where I had not designed nor
> wished.   For all that, I cannot clean myself of
> it. [37]

Thus the author seems to imply that Richard's usurpation of
the crown led to the death of the princes and, though he did
not commit the crime, he must share in the blame.   This
follows rather closely Paul Murray Kendall's evaluation of
Richard's role in the most controversial events of his reign. [38]

Among the less successful of the novels dealing with
Richard are two which were written for young adult readers.
These books present opposing views and each fails for a different reason.   Richard III: The Last Plantagenet by Tyler
Whittle is prefaced by a note from the author who declares
that his book "is entirely faithful to the known facts."[39]
Whittle's research is faultless and his novel is indeed historically accurate.   It is also extremely dull, being simply
a retelling of the story from Richard's point of view.   The
author is an Englishman who writes adult novels under the
name of Mark Oliver, and children's books and non-fiction
under the name of Tyler Whittle, and he seems to have had
some difficulty in deciding in which category Richard III belongs.   It was a mistake to try to fit it into all three.

The Song of a Thrush by Katherine Wigmore Eyre
fails for an entirely different reason.   Her research can
surely have gone no deeper than a reading of Shakespeare's
plays about Richard to which she added the seasoning of her
own vivid imagination.

The heroine of the story is Margaret Plantagenet, the
daughter of Clarence, who is sent with her brother to live

with the royal children. She is therefore in a position to
witness the crimes committed by, or for, her wicked uncle,
Richard of Gloucester, her father's murderer.[40] After the
death of Edward IV, the new king, accompanied by his un-
cles Rivers and Grey and a mere dozen henchmen, set out
from Ludlow for London.[41] Richard, who is in London, is
informed that his nephew and his tiny band are approaching
Stony Stratford where they will spend the night.[42] He and
his henchmen hurry to Stony Stratford where they truss and
gag Rivers and Grey, drag them out of the inn, throw them
across horses, and carry them to Pontefract.[43] Vaughn
seems to have been overlooked by the zealous henchmen,
for he is discovered the following month, plotting with Richard himself.[44]

Richard, the wicked uncle, having dealt with his most
dangerous enemies, swears an oath that his brother Edward's
children are illegitimate, attaints the two young princes, and
throws them into prison.[45] Buckingham refuses Richard's
demand that he murder the princes and decides to support
Henry Tudor,[46] whose plans to seize the throne had been
laid before the death of Edward IV.[47]

The princes cannot be saved, even by this imagina-
tive author, but the villain will reap his just reward. She
describes Richard at the Battle of Bosworth as

> A Crook-Back truly, sitting his mount squat and
> humped.... Thin lips curled in their cold sneer.
> Black eyes glittering, implacable. And around his
> helmet, shining arrogantly, the narrow gold crown
> of the Annointed.[48]

During the battle, Northumberland charges down the hill in
an attempt to save Richard, but to no avail.[49] The battle
ends as it must, no matter who writes the story, with Richard's death and Henry's crowning.

Two other romantic novels written for young adults,
and both favorable to Richard, deserve only slight notice.
Song for a Lute by Marguerite Vance is a superficial account
of Richard's boyhood and reign which concerns itself mainly
with his romance with Anne Neville. Both the chronology
and historical facts are frequently in error. These same
faults are present to an even greater degree in Olive
Eckerson's The Golden Yoke: A Novel of the War of the
Roses, which labors under the additional burden of the author's flowery, cliché-ridden style.

Two other novels which fall easily, but not necessarily, into the young adult category are well-researched
and better written than the two just noted.   Richard, although
a secondary character, is favorably treated in each.   Richard Broome, the king's bastard son, is the hero of Margaret
Campbell Barnes's novel, The King's Bed, and the author
makes use of the story, found in J. H. Jesse's Memoirs of
the Court of England, of Richard's camp bed which remained
at the Blue Boar Inn in Leicester when the royal army left
for Bosworth.   Barnes has written several novels dealing
with this period and, although her dialogue is stilted, she
has managed to weave fact and fiction together without greatly sacrificing either accuracy or plot.

The action of White Rose and Ragged Staff by Elizabeth Seibert takes place, as one might surmise, between
1469 and 1471 during Warwick's rebellion when Henry VI regained, and then finally lost his throne to Edward IV.   The
main plot concerns the romance between one of Richard's
squires and a lady-in-waiting to Anne Neville, who are
caught on opposite sides of the struggle.   Richard is an almost shadowy figure in this romance which ends, as ro-
mances should, happily for all the lovers.

Richard is accorded understanding, but little sympathy,
by Francis Leary in his interesting, but verbose novel, Fire
and Morning, the third part of a trilogy about the Wars of
the Roses.   The author views Richard as a hard, cold man,
but a just and efficient king, and the last one to uphold the
best of the chivalric ideals of knighthood and honor.

Leary's explanation of the murder of the princes is
similar to Kendall's, but rather more vehement.   After fitting together the pieces of the puzzle, the hero of the novel
comes to the realization that

> the dread killer of Edward's sons, the Princes of
> York, had been Buckingham.   Out of mad, insati-
> able ambition....   Who but Buckingham?   Who but
> Richard's High Constable had both the motive and
> the opportunity?   Who but he had concerted with
> Morton to ruin Richard; to murder the boys and
> throw the blame on Richard?[50]

The little princes were the victims of Buckingham,
Morton, Tudor, and, indirectly, of Richard as well, since
it was he who had put them into the Tower.   It was Rich-

ard himself, however, whom Leary sees as the principal
victim, the object not of murder, but of a deliberate campaign of slander and falsehood. The hero, a man with a
foot in both camps, realizes too late that

> Tudor and Morton were contriving another murder--
> a crime beside which the slaughter of the princes,
> terrible as that had been, was of small import:
> they were plotting to murder truth itself; they
> were setting about to slay the past. [51]

Leary has proved that, just as it is possible to accept at least part of the Tudor tradition and still admire
Richard, one is also able to reject the myth completely and
still dislike its victim.

Elizabeth Woodville and several other members of
her enormous family played significant roles during the
reigns of the Yorkist kings and it is, therefore, not surprising to find them as leading characters in novels dealing
with the period. In several of these works Elizabeth herself is the main character, if not necessarily the heroine.

History has not dealt kindly with the Woodvilles, but
Jan Westcott, in her revisionist novel The White Rose, published in 1969, has done her best to improve their image.
All of her Woodvilles, but especially Anthony, Earl Rivers,
are intelligent, handsome, loyal, virtuous, and unselfish,
and her Richard of Gloucester has stepped directly out of
the pages of More and Shakespeare. Indeed, her scene in
which Hastings is arrested and executed comes directly from
More, [52] although she took from the later Tudor playwrights
and poets the idea that Richard lost the battle of Bosworth
because he murdered his nephews and that Henry Tudor won
because he had God on his side. [53] All of this makes the
publisher's claim that Westcott's novel "is researched so
thoroughly it can stand as a full-fledged biography"[54] sound
a little fatuous.

Elizabeth Woodville is the title character in Maureen
Peters' brief, badly-written novel, The Queen Who Never
Was, a superficial and frequently inaccurate account which
takes Elizabeth from girlhood through the marriage of her
daughter to Henry Tudor. The author is more sympathetic
to Richard of Gloucester than she is to her leading lady,
who is portrayed as a proud, greedy and ambitious climber.

Rosemary Hawley Jarman, in her novel about Elizabeth Woodville, The King's Grey Mare, has "endeavoured to
portray her as the victim of circumstances, no worse
and no better than many others of her time."[55] The
author does indeed evince a strange sort of sympathy for this
woman who claimed, through her mother, descent from a
French water sprite and who used her strange powers, first
to entrap a king into marriage, and then to destroy all those
who resented her family's rise to power.

Elizabeth's two young sons are protected by their
uncle Richard when he takes the crown.   Rumors that the
boys have been murdered by Richard are deliberately spread
by Elizabeth, Morton, and other agents of Henry Tudor, in
order to turn the people against the king.[56] It is not until
Henry VII wears the crown, however, that the boys are
murdered by Tyrell, acting under orders from the new
king.[57] Elizabeth, a woman of remarkably poor judgment,
herself becomes a victim of the man she has helped to seize
the throne.   Henry Tudor strips her of all her goods and
sends her to spend the rest of her days in a convent.[59]

"I believe passionately in Richard's innocence," declared Rosemary Jarman when her first novel, We Speak No
Treason, was published in 1971.[59] The King's Grey Mare,
published two years later, was a variation of the testimonial
to that belief given so eloquently in her earlier work.

We Speak No Treason is Richard's story as told by
three people who knew and loved him.   In the first section,
he is seen through the eyes of his young mistress, the mother of his illegitimate daughter Katherine.   The second section is related by the court fool and the third by one of
Richard's knights who fights for him at Barnet and Bosworth,
and who sets down his story while awaiting execution by Henry Tudor.   The fourth section is again the narrative of the
young mistress who has become a nun at Leicester Convent
where Richard's despoiled body was brought after Bosworth.

Jarman steeped herself in the history of the fifteenth
century and her writings reflect the spirit and flavor of the
age.   Richard would be fortunate indeed if all of the novels
written in an attempt to vindicate him could match her
standard of excellence.   Unfortunately, this is not the case.

Marjorie Bowen's Dickon can serve as an example of
a novel written by an author whose advocacy does her hero's

cause no good. In her preface the author declares that she
has violated no known fact. [60] If she had done her research
more carefully, however, she would doubtless have realized
the extent of her violation. She committed small, careless
errors, such as consistently referring to John Howard, Duke
of Norfolk, as Mowbray, and rather more serious lapses,
such as her scene of the interview between Richard and
Buckingham after the latter's rebellion, [61] an interview which,
of course, never took place. Bowen ignores entirely the
question of the princes and their possible fate, an unusual
oversight in any work on Richard III. The author's senti-
mental style and stilted, artificial dialogue do nothing to re-
deem her book, which cannot be taken seriously either as
history or literature.

In the Shadow of the Tower is the title of a series of
six novels, each written by a different author, and each
dealing in some way with the Wars of the Roses. Richard,
at different stages of his life, is a central character in several of the novels in the series. Richard's courtship of
Anne Neville is the theme of The Warwick Heiress by Margaret Abbey, the nom de plume of Margaret York, the chairman of the Leicester branch of the Richard III Society.
Richard is portrayed as a reserved, but kind young man who
is handicapped by a severe limp. Bits of the Tudor myth
crop up, it seems, even in books written by Society members. The novel is, however, quite well-written and researched and the author has succeeded in the difficult task
of bringing Richard's personality to life.

Richmond and Elizabeth by Brenda Honeyman is really
Elizabeth of York's story, but quite naturally, her uncle
Richard plays an important part in it. It is Honeyman's
contention that Elizabeth was deeply in love with Richard and
would have married him willingly, after the death of his
wife, had he asked her. On the contrary, he publicly dis-
claimed any such intention, to the great relief of Henry Tudor. [62]

Honeyman believes that the princes were indeed murdered during Richard's reign, but not on his orders or with
his consent. Catesby and Ratcliffe were responsible for the
crime. [63] Henry's execution of Tyrell and the publication of
his secret confession in Vergil's Historia, both of which took
place many years after the murder, were dictated, this author declares, by Henry's fears of an uprising in the
princes's favor after the death of his elder son, Arthur. [64]

Honeyman writes well, and she has done her research
thoroughly.   Her conclusions will not be universally accepted,
but her balanced treatment of the personalities on both sides
of the conflict must be considered fair to all concerned.

Richard III is an enigma, and his role, if he played
one, in the death of the princes, is a puzzle.   Here indeed
are the essential ingredients for a mystery story and three
very skillful writers have used them to create three totally
different novels.

The earliest and, no doubt the most influential, of
the Ricardian mystery novels is Josephine Tey's The Daughter of Time.   It is probably no exaggeration to say that if
Shakespeare presented the most damning case for the prose-
cution against Richard III, Josephine Tey has countered with
the most persuasive argument for the defense.   She refuses
to pay respectful lip service to even the most revered of the
opposition writers.   The detective hero of the novel, lying
in a hospital bed, reviews the evidence against Richard, at
first merely as something to pass the time, and then with
an increasing sense of mission.   He finds himself repelled
by the "aroma of back-stairs gossip and servant's spying"
which emanated from the pages of More's History. 65   The
"honest, learned, and, according to his lights impartial"66
Gairdner fares no better than More.   "The spectacle of Dr.
Gairdner trying to make his facts fit his theory was the
most entertaining thing in gymnastics"67 that Tey's detective
had ever seen.   Gairdner does possess one virtue not found
in More.   "He was as honest as the day.   He just couldn't
reason from B to C. "68

Tey refutes More, Gairdner, and the other traditionalists with logical, deductive reasoning.   Richard, she declares, was a logical men who did not do anything without
a reason.   There was no reason for him to murder his
nephews and it would, therefore, have been a useless, silly
crime, and Richard was not a silly man.   It was a cruel,
heartless murder, and Richard was a warm-hearted man.
"One could go through the catalogue of his acknowledged
virtues, and find that each of them, individually, made his
part in the murder unlikely in the extreme.   Taken together
they amounted to a wall of impossibility that towered into
fantasy. "69

Henry Tudor, on the other hand, while also not a
silly man, was cold-hearted and cruel when his policy de-

manded that he be so. Since even the Tudor historians concede that under Henry VII and Henry VIII all the remaining
Yorkist claimants to the throne were judicially murdered,
Tey is convinced that the two princes were the first victims of the Tudors. Tyrell's confession, made twenty years
after the murders and before his own execution, she sees as
patently fraudulent and further proof of Henry's rather than
Richard's guilt. [70]

Josephine Tey was a respected and popular novelist,
and the clarity and enthusiasm with which she expounded her
views about Richard III have caused many readers to reevaluate one of the traditional, and therefore cherished,
myths of history.

Jeremy Potter, the chairman of the London branch of
the Richard III Society, takes an entirely different approach
to the mystery of the princes in the Tower. In the author's
note which precedes his mystery novel, A Trail of Blood, he
acknowledges his debt to Paul Murray Kendall for the facts
and to Josephine Tey for the inspiration of his work. He
further declares:

> Ever since their supposed murder the princes in
> the Tower have haunted English history. The ques-
> tion of Richard III's guilt has been debated for
> nearly five hundred years. All I claim for my
> version of events is that it is as plausible as the
> one circulated by three earlier practitioners of the
> art of crime fiction: H. Tudor, T. More, and W.
> Shakespeare.

The story takes place in the reign of Henry VIII, during the Pilgrimage of Grace, the northern rebellion in protest of the suppression of the monasteries. Robert Aske
and a chancellor of the Bishop of Lincoln have come to
Croyland Abbey to search the chronicles and records in order
to find a Plantagenet leader who will defend the old faith and
save the monasteries. The search leads to the discovery
that the princes had escaped an attempted assassination by
agents of Buckingham, but that Edward had drowned during
the flight. Richard, whose identity is discovered, refuses
to continue the civil war to retrieve the crown and the rebellion fails. In explanation of his refusal to lead a Yorkist
uprising he says:

> Ruthlessness is the stamp of a successful ruler.

> My uncle King Richard was a good man. He in-
> tended well but committed the error of showing
> mercy to his enemies. He spared the lives of
> those who conspired against him and left them
> their liberty to bring him down. The quality of
> mercy cost him his throne and his life. Henry
> Tudor showed no such weakness. For all his
> bastard blood he was a real king. 71

Excellent plotting and a good narrative style place
this novel well above the usual run of mystery stories. It
can fit quite comfortably alongside of Josephine Tey's classic.

The Murders of Richard III by Elizabeth Peters is
set in the English country house party so frequently employed
as background by writers of mystery novels. This house
party, however, is not the usual sort. The guests, all
members of a splinter group of the Richard III Society, have
gathered to see the original letter, mentioned by Buck, which
Elizabeth of York wrote to Norfolk, telling of her love for
her uncle Richard. Each of the guests is dressed as an important character in Richard's life and, one by one, each becomes the victim of a recreation of the death of the original
character. Beheading, poisoning, smothering, and drowning
in a butt of malmsey are all attempted as the culprit goes
through the list of the murders attributed to Richard. The
author of this cleverly written book pokes gentle fun at her
fellow Ricardians, but she manages nevertheless, to include
all of their arguments in defense of Richard.

Other novels have been, and no doubt will continue to
be written about Richard III and the many roles he played
during a brief, but adventurous life. * Quite obviously, the
materials exist for many variations if an author has the in-
genuity and skill to utilize them. Speculation must necessarily be a part of any historical novel, but it should never
be at variance with fact. Most novelists do not pretend to
be historians, but since it is quite likely that most people
remember the "history" they read in fiction more vividly
than what they learned from history books, it is incumbent
upon an author to do careful research and to use the results
honestly.

---

*See the Bibliography of Fiction which includes titles of
novels not discussed in this work.

Eight

CONCLUSION

When Richard III died at Bosworth Field on August 22, 1485, he was not quite thirty-three years old, and his reign, one of the shortest in English history, had endured for little more than two years. Had he been able to keep his throne for another twenty or thirty years, would the course of English or American history have been appreciably different? One might speculate endlessly on this question, but the answer can, of course, never be known. It is not difficult to imagine, however, that had Henry Tudor lost the day, and his life, the incident would probably have been recorded as no more than another attempt by a penniless adventurer to seize a crown, and as such, would scarcely merit more than a footnote in history books. Richard III, however, would no doubt enjoy a vastly improved reputation. Even had he been the murderer of his nephews, it is possible that, granted a long and prosperous reign, men would have been inclined to forgive, or at least minimize, his transgressions. Henry VIII, for example, does not come off too badly at the hands of historians, but how would he have fared had he died immediately after his marriage to Jane Seymour? A long period of Yorkist domination undoubtedly would have ensured the same sympathetic treatment accorded the Tudors at the hands of contemporary historians, and the genius of Vergil, More, and Shakespeare might well have been employed in fashioning a Yorkist, rather than a Tudor legend.

Historians, like all men, are shaped by their experiences, background, and the age in which they live, and they must, of necessity, view both the present and past through a veil of their own values and prejudices. The responsible historian recognizes this and strives to minimize, though he may not be able to eliminate, the distortion caused by his bias. His predilections show themselves not only in the interpretation of facts, but also in his selection of which facts he will note and record, and which he will discard or ignore.

This is equally true of the contemporary chronicler who
wrote from personal eye-witness knowledge and the later
historian who used these primary sources to write his own
version of events and the personalities who shaped them.

If one accepts that historical bias is indeed a fact,
questions regarding the accuracy of the written history of the
Yorkist period necessarily arise.   Were the Tudor historians, as has frequently been charged, more than ordinarily
biased, and did they willfully distort what they knew to be
the truth?   Did they, in fact, deliberately invent the history
of the late fifteenth century to suit their Tudor masters?
These questions, like others concerning what Paul Murray
Kendall has termed the "Great Debate," cannot be answered
with any degree of certainty.   There may indeed have been
an attempt by some of these writers, both historians and
playwrights, to curry favor or heighten the drama of the
story by exaggeration or deliberate invention, but it is quite
probable that most of them really believed that what they
wrote was the truth.   This is not to say, of course, that it
was the truth, but only that it was accepted as such.   The
few contemporary documents relating to the Yorkist reigns
were unknown to most writers of the succeeding century, but
it is unlikely, in any event, in an age when standards of historical judgment were as yet unformed, that such sources
would have been valued as highly as they later came to be.

A point which has frequently been stressed by Richard's defenders and accepted by those historians who have
sought to maintain a balanced perspective, is one which has
been largely ignored or denied by writers who can find no
flaw in the Tudor tradition.   The point is that Henry Tudor
and Bishop Morton had an obvious interest in encouraging
the view that Richard's reign was illegal and immoral, and
they were in a position of power which enabled them to influence popular opinion and propagate their own views.

If one can excuse, or at least understand, the distortions, inventions, and inaccuracies of Vergil, More,
Shakespeare, and the others who helped to create the Tudor
legend, on the grounds of ignorance or expediency, what
reasons can explain the acceptance by later historians of this
largely discredited version of history?   Why have distinguished scholars such as Gairdner and Rowse chosen to believe stories which have been shown to have little or no
basis in fact?   Various theories have been offered to explain this apparent contradiction between great scholarship

and uncritical acceptance of tradition.   Any explanation of the
historian's bias, whether it be Gairdner's on the one side,
or Markham's on the other, must take into account the experiences which shaped it.

      The central point of the controversy surrounding
Richard III, the mystery of the fate of the princes, will,
no doubt, continue to be the subject of endless debate.
Richard may indeed have been responsible for their deaths.
It has not been, and cannot be proven.   Nevertheless, as
Jacob and Kendall have pointed out, Richard's case is somewhat damaged by the fact that the princes disappeared during
his reign and no record exists of their having been seen
afterward.   On the other hand, no evidence links Richard to
the alleged murders of Prince Edward, Henry VI, Clarence,
or Anne and these tales, like Richard's supposed deformity,
must be termed fantasy.   They will, no doubt, continue to
be repeated as historical fact.   Tradition plays a significant
part in the history of any people, but blind acceptance of
tradition does no service to the study of history.

CHAPTER NOTES

CHAPTER TWO

1 For the account which follows the author has re-
lied heavily on Richard the Third by Paul Murray Kendall
(New York: Doubleday, 1956). For other good surveys of
the period see also The Fifteenth Century by E. F. Jacob
(Oxford: Clarendon Press, 1961) and Richard the Third by
James Gairdner (Cambridge, England: Cambridge University
Press, 1898).
2 Kendall, Richard III, p. 29.
3 Ibid., pp. 29-31.
4 Ibid., p. 34.
5 Ibid., p. 36.
6 Hearne's Fragment in Chronicles of the White
Rose of York, ed. by J. C. Giles (London: James Bohn,
1843), pp. 5-6.
7 Kendall, Richard III, p. 37.
8 Ibid., pp. 37-38.
9 Ibid., p. 39.
10 Ibid., pp. 39-40.
11 See the statements of two contemporaries, William
Wyrcester and Whethamstede, as quoted in Chronicles of the
White Rose of York, p. lxxx.
12 Ibid., pp. lxxxi-lxxxii.
13 Kendall, Richard III, p. 42.
14 For the quote from Wyrcester, see Chronicles of
the White Rose of York, p. lxxxiii.
15 Ingulph's Chronicle of the Abbey of Croyland, ed.
and transl. by Henry T. Riley (London: Henry G. Bohn,
1854), pp. 421-422.
16 Kendall, Richard III, p. 44.
17 Croyland Chronicle, p. 424.
18 Ibid., pp. 425-426.
19 Kendall, Richard III, p. 49.
20 Ibid., p. 51.

21 Ibid. , p. 52.
22 Ibid. , pp. 55-56.
23 Croyland Chronicle, pp. 439-440.
24 Kendall, Richard III, pp. 58-59.
25 Croyland Chronicle, p. 445.
26 Hearne's Fragment in Chronicles of the White
Rose of York, p. 23.
27 Ibid. , p. 25.
28 Kendall, Richard III, pp. 87-88.
29 Ibid. , p. 89.
30 Ibid. , pp. 90-91.
31 Ibid. , pp. 94-95.
32 Hearne's Fragment in Chronicles of the White
Rose of York, pp. 26-27.
33 Kendall, Richard III, p. 98.
34 "The Manner and Guiding of the Earl of Warwick
at Angers" in Ellis's Original Letters, second series, Vol.
1 (London: Harding & Lepard, 1827), pp. 132-135.
35 Croyland Chronicle, p. 462.
36 Ibid. , p. 463.
37 Historie of the Arrivall of Edward IV. in England,
and the finall recoverye of his kingdomes from Henry VI. ,
ed. by John Bruce (London: Camden Society, 1838), p. 4.
38 Ibid. , pp. 10-11.
39 Ibid. , p. 18.
40 Ibid. , p. 20.
41 Ibid. , p. 30.
42 Ibid. , p. 38.
43 Kendall, Richard III, pp. 124-125.
44 Croyland Chronicle, pp. 469-470.
45 Ibid. , p. 470.
46 Kendall, Richard III, p. 127.
47 Ibid. , p. 130.
48 Phillippe de Commynes, The Memoirs of
Phillippe de Commynes, ed. by Samuel Kinser, transl. by
Isabelle Cazeaux (2 vols. , Columbia: University of South
Carolina Press, 1969), I, p. 264.
49 Croyland Chronicle, p. 471.
50 Kendall, Richard III, pp. 133-134.
51 Commynes, Memoirs, I, p. 282.
52 Croyland Chronicle, p. 478.
53 Kendall, Richard III, pp. 145-146.
54 Ibid. , p. 146.
55 Ibid. , p. 147.
56 Croyland Chronicle, pp. 479-480.
57 Dominic Mancini, The Usurpation of Richard the
Third, ed. by C. A. J. Armstrong (2nd ed. , Oxford:
Clarendon Press, 1969), p. 63.

58   Kendall, Richard III, p. 149.
59   James Gairdner, Richard the Third (Cambridge,
England: Cambridge University Press, 1898), p. 42.
60   Kendall, Richard III, pp. 158-159.
61   Croyland Chronicle, p. 481.
62   Kendall, Richard III, p. 170.
63   Ibid., p. 176.

CHAPTER THREE

1   Croyland Chronicle, p. 483.
2   Ibid., p. 484.
3   Sir Thomas More, The History of King Richard
III, in The Complete Works of St. Thomas More, ed. by
Richard S. Sylvester, vol. II (New Haven: Yale University
Press, 1963), p. 13.
4   Mancini, The Usurpation of Richard III, pp. 71, 73.
5   Croyland Chronicle, p. 485.
6   Mancini, The Usurpation of Richard III, p. 73.
7   Kendall, Richard III, p. 194.
8   Ibid., p. 195.
9   Croyland Chronicle, p. 486.
10   Kendall, Richard III, p. 196.
11   Ibid., pp. 197-198.
12   Ibid., p. 200.
13   Ibid., p. 201.
14   Mancini, The Usurpation of Richard III, p. 73.
15   Kendall, Richard III, p. 203.
16   Croyland Chronicle, p. 486.
17   Ibid., p. 487.
18   Kendall, Richard III, p. 212.
19   Croyland Chronicle, pp. 486-487.
20   More, History of King Richard III, p. 21.
21   Croyland Chronicle, pp. 487-488.
22   Ibid.
23   Kendall, Richard III, p. 235.
24   Ibid., pp. 223-224.
25   This is Kendall's analysis of Buckingham's influence and position during the Protectorship. See ibid., pp.
227-228.
26   Kendall, Richard III, p. 243.
27   York Records as quoted by Kendall, Richard III,
p. 245.
28   Croyland Chronicle, p. 488.
29   Kendall, Richard III, p. 449.

30   Ibid., p. 250.
31   Croyland Chronicle, p. 489.
32   Ibid., pp. 488-489.
33   Ibid., p. 489.
34   Kendall, Richard III, pp. 259-260.   See also
Gairdner, Richard III, pp. 91-92, and Sharon Turner, The
History of England During the Middle Ages, vol. III (3rd ed.,
London: Longman, Rees, et al., 1830), pp. 326-327.
35   Kendall, Richard III, pp. 263-264.
36   Croyland Chronicle, pp. 489-490.
37   Kendall, Richard III, p. 302.
38   Croyland Chronicle, pp. 490-491.
39   Kendall, Richard III, p. 320.
40   Croyland Chronicle, p. 491.
41   Kendall, Richard III, p. 324.
42   Polydore Vergil, English History, ed. by Sir
Henry Ellis (London: Camden Society, 1844), p. 199.
43   Ibid., p. 200.
44   Croyland Chronicle, p. 492.
45   Ibid., p. 495.
46   Vergil, English History, p. 204.
47   Croyland Chronicle, p. 495.
48   Kendall, Richard III, p. 343.
49   Croyland Chronicle, p. 496.
50   Vergil, English History, pp. 210, 214.
51   Croyland Chronicle, p. 496.
52   Kendall, Richard III, pp. 349-350.
53   Croyland Chronicle, pp. 499-500.
54   Ibid., p. 497.
55   Ibid., p. 501.
56   Vergil, English History, p. 216.
57   William Hutton, The Battle of Bosworth Field,
ed. and with additions by J. Nichols (2nd ed., London:
Nichols, Son, and Bentley, 1813), pp. 25-27.
58   Ibid., pp. 83-84.
59   Vergil, English History, p. 217.
60   Croyland Chronicle, pp. 501-502.
61   Kendall, Richard III, pp. 420-421.
62   Vergil, English History, pp. 222-223.
63   Kendall, Richard III, p. 427.   See also Albert
Makinson, "The Road to Bosworth Field," History Today,
vol. 13, no. 4 (April 1963), in which the author discusses
the possibility that the mechanics of the battle, and Northumberland's position in the rear, made it impossible for
him to come to Richard's aid in time (p. 247).   The fact
that Northumberland submitted quickly to Henry, however,
suggests both the possibility of treachery and that the out-

come of the battle did not displease Northumberland (p. 249).
   64 Croyland Chronicle, p. 503.
   65 Kendall, Richard III, pp. 433-434.
   66 Ibid., p. 434.
   67 Ibid., pp. 435-436. Hutton in Bosworth Field
gives as the figures: Henry, more than 7000; Lord Stanley,
5000; Sir William Stanley, 3000; and Richard, 12,000 (p. 75).
   68 Hutton, Bosworth Field, pp. 107-108.
   69 Kendall, Richard III, pp. 439-440.
   70 Hutton, Bosworth Field, p. 111.
   71 Vergil, English History, p. 224.
   72 Croyland Chronicle, p. 504.
   73 Kendall, Richard III, p. 553.

CHAPTER FOUR

   1 J. R. Lander, The Wars of the Roses (New York:
G. P. Putnam's Sons, 1965), p. 13.
   2 Ibid.
   3 This manuscript was transcribed by John Stow
from a copy in the possession of the Recorder of London,
Fleetwood.
   4 Chronicles of the White Rose, p. 97.
   5 Charles Lethbridge Kingsford, English Historical
Literature in the Fifteenth Century (Oxford: Clarendon Press,
1913), pp. 181-182.
   6 Ibid., p. 184, and Kendall, Richard III, p. 469.
   7 Arrivall of Edward IV, p. 30.
   8 John Warkworth, A Chronicle of the First Thirteen
Years of the Reign of King Edward the Fourth, ed. by James
Orchard-Halliwell (London: Camden Society, 1838), p. 18.
   9 Croyland Chronicle, p. 466.
   10 Arrivall of Edward IV, p. 38.
   11 Ibid.
   12 Ibid.
   13 Warkworth, Chronicle, p. 21.
   14 Croyland Chronicle, p. 468.
   15 Ibid.
   16 Commynes, Memoirs, I, 9.
   17 Ibid., pp. 16, 18.
   18 Ibid., p. 123.
   19 Ibid., p. 16.
   20 C. A. J. Armstrong, ed., The Usurpation of
Richard III. by Dominic Mancini, p. 4.

21 Ibid., p. 20.
22 Ibid., p. 18.
23 Ibid., p. 16.
24 Mancini, The Usurpation of Richard III, p. 59.
25 Armstrong, ed., ibid., p. 19.
26 Commynes, Memoirs, p. 225.
27 Ibid.
28 Croyland Chronicle, pp. 478-480.
29 Mancini, The Usurpation of Richard III, p. 63.
30 Ibid.
31 Commynes, Memoirs, pp. 122-123, and Chronicles
of the White Rose, p. 251.
32 Commynes, Memoirs, pp. 122-123.
33 See above, pp. 39-40.
34 Croyland Chronicle, p. 485.
35 Ibid., p. 488.
36 Ibid.
37 Mancini, The Usurpation of Richard III, pp. 89,
91.
38 Alison Hanham, "Richard III, Lord Hastings and
the Historians," English Historical Review (April 1972), p.
238.
39 Ibid., pp. 242, 248.
40 Ibid., p. 248. Hanham has included these arguments in her recently published full-length work Richard III
and His Early Historians 1483-1525 (Oxford: Clarendon
Press, 1975), in which she also discusses The Croyland
Chronicle, the works of More, Vergil, and Mancini, and
other, lesser writers of the period.
41 Croyland Chronicle, p. 488.
42 Ibid., p. 489.
43 Mancini, The Usurpation of Richard III, pp. 91,
93.
44 Commynes, Memoirs, II, p. 414.
45 Ibid.
46 Armstrong, ed., The Usurpation of Richard III
by Mancini, pp. 17-18.
47 Commynes, Memoirs, I, pp. 367-368.
48 Mancini, The Usurpation of Richard III, p. 91.
49 Ibid., p. 99.
50 See above, p. 34.
51 Mancini, The Usurpation of Richard III, p. 93.
52 Ibid.
53 Armstrong, ed., The Usurpation of Richard III,
pp. 22-23.
54 Kendall, Richard III, p. 468.
55 Mancini, The Usurpation of Richard III, pp. 83,
85.

56   Ibid., pp. 63, 65.
57   Croyland Chronicle, p. 491.
58   Ibid.
59   Ibid., p. 498.
60   Ibid., p. 499.
61   Ibid., p. 504.
62   Ibid.
63   Kendall, Richard III, p. 512, Kingsford, English
Historical Literature, p. 184, and Sir Clements Markham,
Richard III: His Life and Character (Bath, England: Cedric
Chivers, 1968), pp. 175-177.
64   Kendall, Richard III, p. 512.
65   Croyland Chronicle, p. 504.
66   Hanham, Richard III and His Early Historians, p.
100.
67   Armstrong, ed., The Usurpation of Richard III,
p. 137.
68   Ibid., pp. 137-138. See also Kendall, Richard
III, p. 537, n. 26.
69   York City Records, as quoted by Jean Heneage
Jesse, Memoirs of the Court of England: King Richard the
Third and Some of His Contemporaries (Boston: Chester F.
Rice, n.d.), p. 289.
70   Kendall, Richard III, pp. 496-497.
71   Kingsford, English Historical Literature, p. 185.
72   John Rous, Rous Rolls, as quoted by V. B.
Lamb, The Betrayal of Richard III (4th ed., London: Mitre
Press, 1972), p. 58.
73   Kendall, Richard III, p. 497.
74   A. R. Myers, "Richard III and Historical Tradition," History, 53 (1968), p. 183.
75   Rous, Rous Roll, as quoted by Kendall, Richard
III, p. 497.
76   Lamb, The Betrayal of Richard III, pp. 59-60.
77   Kingsford, English Historical Literature, p. 185.
78   Kendall, Richard III, pp. 497-498.
79   Sir Henry Ellis, ed., English History, by
Polydore Vergil (London: Camden Society, 1844), p. xx.
80   Kingsford, English Historical Literature, p. 254.
81   Ellis, ed., Polydore Vergil's English History,
p. xx, and Kingsford, English Historical Literature, p. 191.
82   Ellis, ed., Polydore Vergil's English History,
p. xxiii, and Kendall, Richard III, p. 502.
83   Philip Lindsay, The Tragic King: Richard III
(New York: Robert M. McBride, 1934), p. 233.
84   Polydore Vergil, English History, p. 152.
85   Kingsford, English Historical Literature, p. 191.
86   Vergil, English History, p. 152.

87   Robert Fabyan, The New Chronicles of England and France, ed. by Henry Ellis (London: F. C. and J. Rivington, et al., 1811), p. 622.

88   Ibid.
89   Vergil, English History, p. 156.
90   Fabyan, Chronicles, p. 670.
91   Ibid.
92   Ibid.
93   Vergil, English History, p. 180.
94   Ibid., p. 173.
95   Ibid.
96   Ibid., p. 175.
97   Ibid., pp. 177-178.
98   Ibid., pp. 180-181.
99   Ibid., pp. 183-184.
100   Ibid., pp. 184-185.
101   Ibid., p. 186.
102   Ibid., pp. 187-188.
103   Ibid., p. 188.
104   Myers, "Richard III and Historical Tradition," p. 184.
105   Kendall, Richard III, pp. 498-499.
106   Henry Ellis, ed., The Chronicle of John Hardyng together with the Continuation of Richard Grafton (London: F. C. & J. Rivington, et al., 1812), p. xix.
107   Kendall, Richard III, p. 499.
108   Ibid.
109   Paul Murray Kendall, ed., Richard III: The Great Debate (New York: W. W. Norton, 1965), pp. 24-25.
110   Kendall, Richard III, p. 500.
111   Ibid., pp. 500-501.
112   More, History of King Richard III, pp. 7-8.
113   Ibid., p. 48.
114   Ibid., p. 8.
115   Ibid.
116   Ibid.
117   George Ferrers, "George, Duke of Clarence," in The Mirror for Magistrates, ed. by Lily B. Campbell (Cambridge, England: Cambridge University Press, 1938), p. 234.
118   More, History of King Richard III, pp. 54-55.
119   Ibid., p. 59.
120   Ibid., pp. 64-65.
121   Lamb, The Betrayal of Richard III, p. 91.
122   Kendall, Richard III, pp. 554-555 n.
123   More, History of King Richard III, p. 83.
124   Ibid., p. 82.

125 Ibid., pp. 85-86.
126 For a complete discussion of More's version of
the death of the princes see Kendall's Richard III, Appendix
I.
127 More, History of King Richard III, p. 86.
128 Richard Grafton, Continuation of Hardyng's
Chronicle, p. 537.
129 Kingsford, English Historical Literature, p. 261.
130 Edward Hall, Chronicles, ed. by Sir Henry
Ellis (London: J. Johnson; F. C. & J. Rivington, et al.,
1809), p. 407.
131 Ibid., p. 415.
132 Ibid., p. 416.
133 Ibid.
134 Ibid., pp. 416-417.
135 Ibid., p. 421.
136 Raphael Holinshed, Chronicles of England, Scotland, and Ireland, ed. by Henry Ellis (London: J. Johnson,
F. C. & J. Rivington, et al., 1808), p. 478.
137 Francis Bacon, History of the Reign of Henry
VII, in The Works of Francis Bacon, vol. I (Philadelphia:
Carey & Hart, 1848), p. 314.
138 Ibid.
139 Ibid., p. 317.
140 Ibid., p. 319.
141 John Trussell, A Continuation of the Collection
of the History of England, etc. (London: printed by M. D.
for Ephraim Dawson, 1636), Introduction.
142 Ibid.
143 Ibid., title page.
144 See above, pp. 12-13.
145 Trussell, Continuation, p. 204.
146 Ibid., pp. 206-207.
147 Ibid., p. 212.
148 Ibid., p. 216.
149 David Hume, The History of England, vol. II
(New York: Harper & Brothers, n.d.), p. 645 n.
150 Ibid., p. 505.
151 Ibid., p. 495.
152 Ibid., p. 465.
153 Ibid., p. 492.
154 Ibid., pp. 450-451.
155 W. Gordon Zeeveld, "A Tudor Defense of Richard III," Publications of the Modern Language Association of
America, 55 (1940), pp. 956-957.
156 Ibid., p. 950.
157 Sir William Cornwallis, "The Prayse of King

Richard the Third," in Essayes of Certaine Paradoxes (London: T. Thorp, 1616), p. B2.

    158 Ibid., p. B3.
    159 Ibid., p. C4.
    160 Ibid.
    161 Ibid., p. E3.
    162 Myers, "Richard III and Historical Tradition,"
p. 185.
    163 A. R. Myers, Introduction to reprint ed. of
The History of the Life and Reigne of Richard III by George
Buck (Wakefield, Yorkshire: EP Publishing, 1973), p. ix.
    164 Ibid.
    165 Kendall, Richard III, p. 506.
    166 Sir George Buck, The History of the Life and
Reigne of Richard III (London: W. Wilson, 1647), p. 76.
    167 Ibid., pp. 76-77.
    168 Ibid., pp. 80-81.
    169 Ibid., p. 116.
    170 Ibid., p. 85.
    171 Ibid., pp. 87-88.
    172 Ibid., p. 130.
    173 Myers, "Richard III and Historical Tradition,"
p. 186.
    174 Horace Walpole, Historic Doubts on the Life and
Reign of Richard the Third (London: Printed for J. Dodsley
in Pall-Mall, 1768), p. 8.
    175 Ibid., pp. 65-66, and Kendall, Great Debate, p.
147.
    176 Walpole, Historic Doubts, p. XIV.
    177 Ibid., p. 128.
    178 Ibid., pp. 130-132.
    179 Kendall, Great Debate, pp. 149-150.

CHAPTER FIVE

    1 John Lingard and Hilaire Belloc, The History of
England, vol. IV (New York: Catholic Publication Society
of America, 1912), p. 189.
    2 Ibid., pp. 191-192.
    3 Ibid., pp. 210-211.
    4 Ibid., p. 260.
    5 Ibid., pp. 229-230.
    6 Ibid., p. 241.
    7 Ibid., p. 253.

8 See above, p. 53, n. †.
9 Lingard, History of England, pp. 252-253.
10 Ibid., p. 260.
11 Sharon Turner, The History of England During the Middle Ages, vol. III (3rd ed., London: Longman, Rees, et al., 1830), p. 313 n.
12 Ibid., book 4, chapter iv.
13 Ibid.
14 Ibid.
15 Ibid., pp. 326-327.
16 Ibid., p. 345.
17 Ibid., p. 345 n.
18 Ibid., p. 362.
19 Ibid., pp. 348-349.
20 Ibid., p. 423.
21 Ibid., p. 449.
22 Ibid., p. 462.
23 Ibid., p. 488.
24 Ibid., pp. 530-531.
25 John Heneage Jesse, Memoirs of the Court of England: King Richard the Third and Some of His Contemporaries (Boston: Chester F. Rice, n.d.), p. 60.
26 Ibid., p. 88.
27 Ibid., p. 97.
28 Ibid., pp. 112-114.
29 Ibid., pp. 132-133.
30 Ibid., pp. 134-135.
31 Ibid., p. 184.
32 Ibid., p. 229.
33 Caroline A. Halsted, Richard III. as Duke of Gloucester and King of England (Philadelphia: Carey & Hart, 1844), p. 47.
34 Ibid., p. 48.
35 Ibid., pp. 75-76.
36 Ibid., p. 213.
37 Ibid., pp. 235-236.
38 Ibid., chapter xiv.
39 Alfred O. Legge, The Unpopular King: The Life and Times of Richard III (2 vols., London: Ward and Downey, 1885), I, 217.
40 Ibid., p. 209.
41 Ibid., p. 220.
42 Ibid., p. 288.
43 Ibid., p. 251.
44 Ibid., p. 280.
45 Ibid., p. 220.
46 Ibid., p. 153.

124   Richard III

47 Ibid., II, 46.
48 Ibid., p. 57.
49 Ibid., pp. 65-66.
50 Ibid., p. 67.
51 Ibid., p. 73.
52 Ibid., p. 290.
53 James Gairdner, Richard the Third (Cambridge, England: Cambridge University Press, 1898), p. x.
54 Ibid., p. xi.
55 Ibid., p. 1.
56 Kendall, Richard III, p. 510.
57 Gairdner, Richard III, p. 12.
58 Ibid., p. 18.
59 Ibid., p. 78.
60 Ibid., p. 115.
61 Ibid., p. 124.
62 Ibid., p. 251.
63 Ibid., p. 247.
64 Ibid., p. 259.
65 Sir Clements Markham, Richard III: His Life and Character (Bath, England: Cedric Chivers, 1968), p. vi.
66 Ibid., p. 24.
67 Sir Clements Markham, "Richard III: A Doubtful Verdict Reviewed," English Historical Review (April 1891), p. 257.
68 Markham, Richard III, p. 172.
69 Ibid., p. 175.
70 See above, pp. 39-40.
71 Markham, Richard III, pp. 177-178.
72 Ibid., pp. 184-185.
73 Ibid., pp. 206-207.
74 Ibid., p. 208.
75 Ibid., pp. 210-211.
76 Ibid., pp. 218-221.
77 Ibid., p. 233.
78 Ibid., p. 235.
79 Ibid., p. 237.
80 Ibid., p. 242.
81 Ibid., pp. 256-257.
82 Ibid., p. 270.
83 James Gairdner, "Did Henry VII Murder the Princes?," English Historical Review (July 1891), p. 447.
84 Ibid., p. 464.
85 Philip Lindsay, The Tragic King: Richard III (New York: Robert M. McBride, 1934), p. xv.
86 Ibid., p. 305.

87 Ibid., pp. xiv-xv.
88 Ibid., pp. xxviii-xxix.
89 Ibid., pp. xxxi-xxxii.
90 Ibid., p. 191.
91 Ibid., p. 281.
92 Ibid., p. 275.
93 Thomas B. Costain, The Last Plantagenets
(New York: Doubleday, 1962), p. 339.
94 Ibid.
95 Ibid., p. 342.
96 Ibid., p. 384.
97 Ibid., p. 392.
98 Ibid., p. 405.
99 Ibid., p. 411.
100 V. B. Lamb, The Betrayal of Richard III, p.
119.
101 Ibid., p. 122.
102 Ibid., p. 119.
103 Ibid., p. 121.
104 Ibid., p. 122.
105 A. L. Rowse, Bosworth Field and the Wars of
the Roses (London: Macmillan, 1966), p. 180, 158.
106 Ibid., p. 195.
107 Ibid., p. 177.
108 Ibid., p. 180.
109 Ibid., p. 170.
110 Ibid., p. 176.
111 Ibid., p. 190.
112 Ibid., p. 258.
113 Ibid., p. 195.
114 Ibid., p. 261.
115 Ibid., p. 289.
116 Ibid., p. 292.
117 Ibid., pp. 194-195.
118 Ibid., p. 250.
119 Winston Churchill, The Birth of Britain, vol. 1
of A History of the English Speaking Peoples (New York:
Dodd, Mead, 1956), p. 482.
120 Ibid., p. 486.
121 S. B. Chrimes, Lancastrians, Yorkists, and
Henry VII (London: Macmillan, 1964), pp. 126-127.
122 Ibid.
123 Ibid., p. 128.
124 Ibid., pp. 133-134.
125 Ibid., pp. 135-136.
126 Ibid., pp. 136-137.
127 Ibid., p. 138.

128 Ibid.
129 Ibid., p. 143.
130 Ibid., p. 145.
131 Ibid., p. 142.
132 E. F. Jacob, The Fifteenth Century (Oxford: Clarendon Press, 1961), p. 645.
133 Ibid., p. 610, p. 629.
134 Ibid., p. 609.
135 Ibid., p. 610.
136 Ibid., pp. 624-625.
137 Ibid., p. 625.
138 Kendall, Richard III, p. 11.
139 Ibid., p. 372.
140 Ibid., p. 373.
141 Ibid., p. 371.
142 Ibid., pp. 370-371.
143 Ibid., p. 244.
144 Ibid., p. 248.
145 Ibid., p. 250.
146 Ibid., p. 251.
147 Ibid., p. 266.
148 Ibid., p. 465.
149 Ibid., p. 470.
150 Ibid., pp. 480-481.
151 Ibid., p. 482.
152 Ibid., p. 483.
153 Ibid., p. 484.
154 Ibid., p. 485.
155 Ibid., p. 486.
156 Ibid., pp. 486-487.
157 Ibid., p. 488.
158 Ibid.
159 Ibid., p. 490.
160 Ibid., p. 495.
161 Charles Ross, Edward IV (Berkeley: University of California Press, 1974), p. 426.
162 Ibid., pp. 425-426.

CHAPTER SIX

1 Kendall, Great Debate, p. 8.
2 Gairdner, Richard III, p. 345.
3 Ibid., p. 347.
4 Ibid., p. 345.

5 Ibid., p. 358.
6 Ibid., p. 362.
7 Ibid., p. 345.
8 Lily B. Campbell, ed., Mirror for Magistrates,
p. 9.
9 Ibid., p. 54.
10 Ibid., pp. 48-49.
11 "King Henry VI," ibid., p. 218.
12 Ferrers, "George, Duke of Clarence," ibid.,
p. 232.
13 Ibid., p. 233.
14 Ibid., p. 227. See also Hall, Chronicles, p.
326, and Heywood, Edward IV, part II, pp. 138-139.
15 Ibid., p. 234.
16 John Dolman, "Lord Hastings," ibid., p. 264.
17 Ibid., p. 276.
18 Ibid., p. 289.
19 Ibid., p. 296.
20 Ibid., p. 289.
21 Thomas Sackville, "Henry, Duke of Buckingham,"
ibid., p. 330.
22 Ibid., p. 335.
23 William Baldwin, "The Poet Collingbourne," ibid.,
p. 357.
24 Fraunces Seager, "Richard, Duke of Gloucester,"
ibid., p. 359.
25 Ibid., p. 362.
26 Ibid., p. 367.
27 Thomas Churchyard, "Shores Wife," ibid., p. 371.
28 Ibid., p. 384.
29 Ibid., See also Heywood, Edward IV, Part II,
above, p. 84, and More, History, p. 54.
30 Richard Niccols, "The Lamentable Lives and
Deaths of the Two young Princes, Edward the fifth, and his
brother Richard Duke of Yorke," in A Winter Night's Vision
(London: Felix Kyngston, 1610), p. 735.
31 Niccols, "The Tragical Life and Death of King
Richard the Third," ibid., p. 751.
32 Ibid., p. 766.
33 [Christopher Brooke], Ghost of Richard III (London: Shakespeare Society, 1844), title page.
34 Ibid., p. vi.
35 Ibid., p. 17.
36 Ibid.
37 Ibid., p. 18.
38 Ibid., p. 27.
39 Ibid., p. 38.

40 Ibid., p. 62.
41 Ibid., p. 63.
42 Ibid., p. 70.
43 The True Tragedy of Richard III (London: Shakespeare Society, 1844), p. viii.
44 Ibid., p. 25.
45 Ibid., pp. 54-55.
46 Ibid., p. 5.
47 Ibid., p. 65.
48 Ibid., p. 57.
49 Ibid., p. 71n.
50 Thomas Heywood, Edward IV, Part II (London: Shakespeare Society, 1842), p. vii.
51 Ibid., p. 138.
52 Ibid., p. 139.
53 Ibid., p. 186.
54 A. R. Myers, "The Character of Richard III," History Today (August 1954), p. 511.
55 Complete Works of Shakespeare, ed. by William Aldis Wright (New York: Doubleday, 1936), p. 36.
56 Ibid., p. 74.
57 Ibid., p. 112.
58 See above, p. 83.
59 Henry VI, Part III, II.
60 Henry VI, Part II, V, i.
61 Henry VI, Part III, V, vi.
62 Richard III, I, ii.
63 Ibid., I, i.
64 Henry VI, Part III, III, ii.
65 Ibid., V, vi.
66 Ibid.
67 Ibid.
68 Richard III, I, i.
69 Ibid., I, iii.
70 Ibid., II, v.
71 Ibid., III, vii.
72 Ibid., IV, ii.
73 Ibid.
74 Ibid.
75 Ibid., V, iii.
76 Ibid.
77 Ibid., IV, iv.
78 Ibid., V, iii
79 Henry VI, Part III, IV, vi.
80 Richard III, V, v.
81 J. Payne Collier, ed., Ghost of Richard III, pp. xii-xiii.

82   Sir John Beaumont, Bosworth Field (London:
printed by Felix Kyngton for Henry Seile, 1629), p. A3.
83   Ibid., p. 4.
84   Ibid., p. 5.
85   Ibid.
86   Ibid., p. 15.
87   Ibid., p. 28.
88   Ibid., p. 30.
89   Samuel Pepys, Diary: 1665-66, ed. by Henry
B. Wheatley (New York: Heritage Press, 1942), p. 91.
90   John Caryll, The English Princess (London:
Thomas Dring, 1667), Prologue.
91   Ibid., I, vi.
92   Ibid.
93   Ibid., II, iii.
94   Ibid., III, i.
95   Ibid., III, vi.
96   Ibid., V, x.

CHAPTER SEVEN

1   Edward Bulwer-Lytton, The Last of the Barons
(New York: Charles Scribner's Sons, 1905), VIII, vii.
2   Ibid., VII, viii.
3   Ibid., IX, vi.
4   Ibid.
5   Ibid., XII, iv.
6   Ibid.
7   Hall, Chronicles, p. 297.
8   Bulwer-Lytton, Last of the Barons, XII, v.
9   Ibid.
10   Ibid., XII, vii.
11   Ibid., XI, ii.
12   Ibid.
13   G. P. R. James, The Woodman (3 vols., London: T. C. Newby, 1849), I, 251-253.
14   Ibid., II, 306.
15   Ibid., p. 233.
16   Ibid., III, 209-210.
17   Robert Louis Stevenson, The Black Arrow (New
York: Saalfield Pub. Co., n.d.), p. 206n.
18   Ibid., p. 254.
19   John Reed Scott, Beatrix of Clare (New York:
Grosset & Dunlap, 1907), pp. 108-110.

20   Ibid., p. 202.
21   Dora Greenwell McChesney, The Confession of Richard Plantagenet (London: Smith, Elder, 1913), p. ix.
22   Ibid., p. xviii.
23   Ibid., pp. 38-39.
24   Ibid., pp. 5-6.
25   Ibid., chapter i.
26   Ibid., chapter iv.
27   Ibid., chapter xii.
28   Ibid., chapter xiii.
29   Ibid., chapter xvi.
30   Ibid., chapter xx.
31   Ibid., chapter xxii.
32   Carola Oman, Crouchback (New York: Henry Holt, 1929), Preface.
33   Patrick Carleton, Under the Hog (New York: E. P. Dutton, 1938), p. 257.
34   Ibid., pp. 482-483.
35   Marian Palmer, The White Boar (New York: Doubleday, 1968), pp. 313-314.
36   See above, p. 98.
37   Palmer, The White Boar, p. 326.
38   See above, p. 72.
39   Tyler Whittle, Richard III: The Last Plantagenet (Philadelphia: Chilton Book Co., 1970), Author's Note.
40   Katherine Wigmore Eyre, The Song of a Thrush (New York: Oxford University Press, 1952), p. 241.
41   Ibid., p. 108.
42   Ibid., p. 117.
43   Ibid., pp. 125-126.
44   Ibid., p. 153.
45   Ibid., p. 158.
46   Ibid., pp. 162-163.
47   Ibid., p. 99.
48   Ibid., p. 227.
49   Ibid., p. 229.
50   Francis Leary, Fire and Morning (New York: G. P. Putnam's Sons, 1957), p. 253.
51   Ibid., pp. 194-195.
52   Jan Wescott, The White Rose (New York: G. P. Putnam's Sons, 1969), chapter xxv.
53   Ibid., chapter xxx.
54   Ibid., dust-cover.
55   Rosemary Hawley Jarman, The King's Grey Mare (New York: Little, Brown, 1973), Foreword.
56   Ibid., Part III.
57   Ibid., Part IV.

58   Ibid.

59   Rosemary Hawley Jarman, We Speak No Treason
(New York: Little, Brown, 1971), dust-cover.

60   Marjorie Bowen, Dickon (London: Hodder &
Stoughton, 1953), Preface.

61   Ibid., chapter viii.

62   Brenda Honeyman, Richmond and Elizabeth (London: Robert Hale, 1970), chapter xv.

63   Ibid., chapter xiii.

64   Ibid., chapter xxix.

65   Josephine Tey, The Daughter of Time (New York:
Macmillan, 1951), p. 64.

66   Ibid., p. 170.

67   Ibid.

68   Ibid., p. 180.

69   Ibid., pp. 171-172.

70   Ibid., chapter xiv.

71   Jeremy Potter, A Trail of Blood (New York:
McCall Pub. Co., 1970), pp. 241-242.

SELECTED NONFICTION BIBLIOGRAPHY

Bacon, Francis, Viscount St. Albans. History of the Reign
    of Henry VII. The Works of Francis Bacon. Vol. 1.
    Philadelphia: Carey & Hart, 1848.

Balchin, Nigel. "Richard 111." British History Illustrated,
    October 1974, pp. 28-47.

Buck, Sir George. The History of the Life and Reigne of
    Richard III. London: W. Wilson, 1647.

Chrimes, S. B. Lancastrians, Yorkists, and Henry VII.
    London: Macmillan & Co., Ltd., 1964.

Chronicles of the White Rose of York. Edited by J. C.
    Giles. London: James Bohn, 1843.

Churchill, Winston B. The Birth of Britain. Vol. 1 of
    A History of the English Speaking Peoples. New York:
    Dodd, Mead, 1956.

Clive, Lady Mary. This Sun of York. London: Macmillan,
    1973.

Commynes, Phillippe de. The Memoirs of Phillippe de
    Commynes. Edited by Samuel Kinser. Translated by
    Isabelle Cazeaux. 2 vols. Columbia: University of
    South Carolina Press, 1969.

[Cornwallis, Sir William.] "The Prayse of King Richard
    the Third." Essays of Certaine Paradoxes. London:
    T. Thorp, 1616.

Costain, Thomas B. The Last Plantagenets. New York:
    Doubleday, 1962.

Ellis, Sir Henry, ed. Original Letters Illustrative of English History. Second series, Vol. 1. London: Harding & Lepard, 1827.

Fabyan, Robert. The New Chronicles of England and France. Edited by Henry Ellis. London: F. C. & J. Rivington, et al., 1811.

Gairdner, James. "Did Henry VII Murder the Princes?" English Historical Review, July 1891, pp. 444-464.

_____. The Houses of Lancaster and York. New York: Charles Scribner's Sons, 1903.

_____. Richard the Third. Cambridge, England: Cambridge University Press, 1898.

Grafton, Richard. The Continuation of Hardyng's Chronicle. Edited by Henry Ellis. London: F. C. & J. Rivington, et al., 1812.

Hall, Edward. Chronicles. Edited by Sir Henry Ellis. London: J. Johnson; F. C. & J. Rivington, et al., 1809.

Halsted, Caroline A. Richard III. as Duke of Gloucester and King of England. Philadelphia: Carey & Hart, 1844.

Hanham, Alison. Richard III and His Early Historians 1483-1535. Oxford: Clarendon Press, 1975.

_____. "Richard III, Lord Hastings and the Historians." English Historical Review, April 1972, pp. 233-248.

Historie of the Arrivall of Edward IV. in England, and the Finall Recoverye of His Kingdomes from Henry VI. A.D. 1471. Edited by John Bruce. London: Camden Society, 1838.

Holinshed, Raphael. Chronicles of England, Scotland, and Ireland. Vol. III. Edited by Henry Ellis. London: J. Johnson, F. C. & J. Rivington, et al., 1808.

Hume, David. The History of England. Vol. II. New York: Harper & Brothers, n.d.

Hutton, William. The Battle of Bosworth Field. Edited

and with additions by J. Nichols.   London: Nichols,
Son, and Bentley, 1813.

Ingulph's Chronicle of the Abbey of Croyland.   Edited and
translated by Henry T. Riley.   London: Henry G.
Bohn, 1854.

Jacob, E. F.   The Fifteenth Century.   Oxford: Clarendon
Press, 1961.

Jesse, John Heneage.   Memoirs of the Court of England:
King Richard the Third and Some of His Contemporaries.
Boston: Chester F. Rice, n. d.

Kendall, Paul Murray.   Richard the Third.   New York:
Doubleday, 1956.

_____, ed.   Richard III: The Great Debate.   New York:
W. W. Norton, 1965.

Kingsford, Charles Lethbridge.   English Historical Literature in the Fifteenth Century.   Oxford: Clarendon
Press, 1913.

_____.   Prejudice and Promise in Fifteenth Century Eng-
land.   London: Frank Cass & Co., Ltd., 1962.

Lamb, V. B.   The Betrayal of Richard III.   4th ed.   London: Mitre Press, 1972.

Lander, J. R.   The Wars of the Roses.   New York: G.
P. Putnam's Sons, 1965.

Legge, Alfred O.   The Unpopular King: The Life and Times
of Richard III.   2 Vols.   London: Ward and Downey,
1885.

Levine, Mortimer.   "Richard III--Usurper or Lawful King?"
Speculum, vol. 34, no. 4 (1959), pp. 391-401.

Lindsay, Philip.   The Tragic King: Richard III.   New
York: Robert M. McBride, 1934.

Lingard, John, and Belloc, Hilaire.   The History of England.   Vol. IV.   New York: Catholic Publication Society of America, 1912.

Makinson, Albert. "The Road to Bosworth Field." History Today, April 1963, pp. 239-249.

Mancini, Dominic. The Usurpation of Richard the Third. Edited by C. A. J. Armstrong. Oxford: 2nd ed. Clarendon Press, 1969.

Markham, Sir Clements. "Richard III: A Doubtful Verdict Reviewed." English Historical Review, April 1891, pp. 250-283.

_____. Richard III: His Life and Character. Bath, England: Cedric Chivers, 1968.

More, Sir Thomas. The History of King Richard the Third. Vol. II of The Complete Works of St. Thomas More. Edited by Richard S. Sylvester. New Haven: Yale University Press, 1963.

Myers, A. R. "The Character of Richard III." History Today, August 1954, pp. 511-521.

_____. Introduction to reprint edition of The History of the Life and Reigne of Richard III by George Buck. Wakefield, Yorkshire: EP Publishing, 1973.

_____. "Richard III and Historical Tradition." History, 53 (1968), pp. 181-202.

Ross, Charles. Edward IV. Berkeley: University of California Press, 1974.

Rowse, A. L. Bosworth Field and the Wars of the Roses. London: Macmillan, 1966.

Trussell, John. A Continuation of the Collection of the History of England. London: Printed by M. D. for Ephraim Dawson, 1636.

Turner, Sharon. The History of England During the Middle Ages. Vol. III, 3rd ed. London: Longman, Rees, et al., 1830.

Vergil, Polydore. English History. Edited by Sir Henry Ellis. London: Camden Society, 1844.

Walpole, Horace, Earl of Orford. Historic Doubts on the

Life and Reign of King Richard III. London: Printed for J. Dodsley in Pall-Mall, 1768.

Warkworth, John. A Chronicle of the First Thirteen Years of the Reign of King Edward the Fourth. Edited by James Orchard-Halliwell. London: Camden Society, 1838.

Woodward, G. W. O. Richard III. London: Pitkin Pictorials, 1972.

Zeeveld, W. Gordon. "A Tudor Defense of Richard III." Publications of the Modern Language Association of America, vol. 55 (1940), pp. 946-957.

BIBLIOGRAPHY OF FICTION
(Titles with * are not discussed herein.)

*Abbey, Margaret. [Margaret York.] Son of York. New
   York: Pinnacle Books, 1971.

_____. The Warwick Heiress. London: Robert Hale,
   1970.

*Ainsworth, William Harrison. The Goldsmith's Wife.
   Philadelphia: Rittenhouse Press, n.d.

Barnes, Margaret Campbell. The King's Bed. Philadelphia:
   Macrae Smith, 1962.

*_____. The Tudor Rose. Philadelphia: Macrae Smith,
   1953.

Beaumont, Sir John. Bosworth Field: With a Taste of the
   Variety of Other Poems. London: printed by Felix
   Kyngston for Henry Seile, 1629.

Bowen, Marjorie. Dickon. London: Hodder & Stoughton,
   Ltd., 1953.

[Brereton, Humphrey.] "The Ballad of Bosworth Field."
   In: Gairdner, James. Richard the Third. Cambridge, England: Cambridge University Press, 1898.

_____. "The Song of the Lady Bessy." In: Gairdner,
   James. Richard the Third. Cambridge, England:
   Cambridge University Press, 1898.

[Brooke, Christopher.] The Ghost of Richard the Third.
   London: Shakespeare Society, 1844.

Bulwer-Lytton, Edward. The Last of the Barons. New
   York: Charles Scribner's Sons, 1905.

Bibliography of Fiction   139

Carleton, Patrick. Under the Hog. New York: E. P.
Dutton, 1938.

Caryll, John. The English Princess; or, The Death of
Richard the III. London: Thomas Dring, 1667.

*Deeping, Warwick. Martin Valliant. New York: Robert
M. McBride, n. d.

Eckerson, Olive. The Golden Yoke. New York: Coward-
McCann, 1961.

*Edwards, Rhoda. Some Touch of Pity. London: Hutchin-
son, 1976.

Eyre, Katherine Wigmore. The Song of a Thrush. New
York: Oxford University Press, 1952.

*Fairburn, Eleanor. The Rose at Harvest End. New York:
Reader's Digest Press, 1975.

*   . The Rose in Spring. New York: Pinnacle Books,
1971.

*Few, Mary Dodgen. Under the White Boar. Atlanta:
Droke House-Hallux, 1971.

*Gaunt, William. The Lady in the Castle. New York:
British Book Centre, 1958.

*Graham, Alice Walworth. The Summer Queen. New York:
Doubleday, 1973.

*Hardy, Blanche. Sanctuary. London: Philip Allan, 1925.

Heywood, Thomas. King Edward IV, Part II. London:
Shakespeare Society, 1842.

Honeyman, Brenda. Richmond and Elizabeth. London:
Robert Hale, 1970.

James, G. P. R. The Woodman. 3 Vols. London: T. C.
Newby, 1849.

Jarman, Rosemary Hawley. The King's Grey Mare. New
York: Little, Brown, 1973.

_____. We Speak No Treason. New York: Little, Brown, 1971.

Leary, Francis. Fire and Morning. New York: G. P. Putnam's Sons, 1957.

McChesney, Dora Greenwell. The Confession of Richard Plantagenet. London: Smith, Elder, 1913.

The Mirror for Magistrates. Edited by Lily B. Campbell. Cambridge, England: Cambridge University Press, 1938.

Niccols, Richard. A Winter Night's Vision. London: Felix Kyngston, 1610.

Oman, Carola. Crouchback. New York: Henry Holt & Co., 1929.

Palmer, Marian. The White Boar. New York: Doubleday, 1968.

*_____. The Wrong Plantagenet. New York: Doubleday, 1972.

Peters, Elizabeth. The Murders of Richard III. New York: Dodd, Mead, 1974.

Peters, Maureen. The Queen Who Never Was. London: Robert Hale, 1972.

*Plaidy, Jean. The Goldsmith's Wife. New York: G. P. Putnam's Sons, 1974.

Potter, Jeremy. A Trail of Blood. New York: McCall Pub. Co., 1970.

Scott, John Reed. Beatrix of Clare. New York: Grosset & Dunlap, 1907.

Seibert, Elizabeth. White Rose and Ragged Staff. Indianapolis: Bobbs-Merrill, 1968.

Shakespeare, William. Henry the Sixth, Part II.

_____. Henry the Sixth, Part III.

_____ . The Tragedy of Richard the Third. [Note: one good edition to use for Shakespeare's plays is: The Complete Works of William Shakespeare, edited by William Aldis Wright (New York: Doubleday, 1936).]

Stevenson, Robert Louis. The Black Arrow. New York: Saalfield Pub. Co., n. d.

Tey, Josephine. [Elizabeth Mackintosh.] The Daughter of Time. New York: Macmillan, 1951.

*Thompson, C. J. S. The Witchery of Jane Shore. London: Grayson & Grayson, 1933.

The True Tragedy of Richard the Third. London: Shakespeare Society, 1844.

Vance, Marguerite. Song for a Lute. New York: E. P. Dutton, 1958.

Westcott, Jan. The White Rose. New York: G. P. Putnam's Sons, 1969.

Whittle, Tyler. Richard III: The Last Plantagenet. Philadelphia: Chilton Book Co., 1970.

INDEX

James, G. P. R.   94-96
Jarman, Rosemary Hawley
    104
Jesse, John Heneage   57-59,
    102
Jonson, Ben   88

Kendall, John   39
Kendall, Paul Murray   32n,
    39, 45, 61, 66, 69-71,
    73, 77n, 100, 102, 107,
    110-111
King Edward IV, Part II
    see Heywood, Thomas
King's Bed see Barnes,
    Margaret Campbell
King's Grey Mare see
    Jarman, Rosemary Hawley
Kingsford, C. L.   32n

Lamb, V. B.   65-66
Landois, Pierre   82
Last of the Barons see
    Bulwer-Lytton, Edward
Leary, Francis   102-103
Legge, Alfred O.   59-60
Leicester   27-28, 30, 48,
    80, 102, 104
Levine, Mortimer   61n, 70n
Lindsay, Philip   64-65
Lingard, John   55-56, 58
Louis XI   9-10, 12-13, 34,
    37
Lovell, Francis   7, 59, 77n,
    100
Lucy, Elizabeth   46, 53, 62,
    86
Ludlow   3-4, 16, 32, 101

McChesney, Dora Greenwell
    97-98, 100
Mancini, Dominic   34-38, 40
March, Edward, Earl of
    see Edward IV
Marches, Council for   14
Marches, Warden of   14-15
Margaret of Anjou   4-6,

9-11, 15, 86, 93
Margaret of Burgundy   3-4,
    10, 14
Markham, Sir Clements   61n,
    62-65, 71, 111
Mary of Burgundy   13, 76
Middleham   7-8, 11-12, 14,
    16, 26
Mirror for Magistrates   74-
    79
More, Sir Thomas   44-47,
    49, 51-62, 64-66, 68, 70-
    72, 75-79, 82-83, 85-86,
    91-92, 103, 106-107, 109-
    110
Mortimer's Cross, Battle of
    6, 53, 85
Morton, John, Bishop of Ely
    21-22, 24-25, 36, 38,
    45, 47, 51-52, 62-65,
    77, 95, 102-104, 110
Murders of Richard III   see
    Peters, Elizabeth
Myers, A. R.   52-53

Neville, Anne   3, 9-12, 23,
    26, 30, 35, 37, 39, 41,
    47-48, 50, 55, 62, 66,
    80, 84-87, 93, 95, 98-
    99, 101, 105, 111
Neville, George   12
Neville, Isobel   8-9
Neville, John, Marquis of
    Montagu   9-10
Neville, Richard see War-
    wick, Earl of
Niccols, Richard   79-80
Norfolk, Dowager Duchess
    of 8
Norfolk, John Howard, Duke
    of   28-29, 30-40, 53n,
    55, 74, 105, 108
Northampton   5, 17-19, 76
Northumberland, Earl of
    see Percy, Henry

Oman, Carola   98-99

York, Cecily Neville,
  Duchess of 3, 5-6, 13,
  23, 44, 46, 55, 58, 61-
  62, 77n, 80, 87
York, Richard, Duke of,
  father of Richard III 3-6,
  44, 46
York, Richard, Duke of,
  son of Edward IV 20, 22,
  36, 44, 53-54, 62, 79,
  96, 107-108